(780) 963-8993

THE AUSTRALIAN Women's Weekly
cooking for diabetes

acp books

contents

The oven temperatures in this book are for conventional ovens; if you have a fan-forced oven, decrease the temperature by 10-20 degrees.

Foreword

Being diagnosed with type 1 or type 2 diabetes is usually quite a shock. When it happened to me, I was horrified, then depressed.

'Why me? Why not my partner who took three teaspoons of sugar in every hot drink he consumed?' I was now faced with a chronic disease, one that affects my life and certainly impacts on my food choices. I had to say a fond farewell to the gorgeous croissants I'd had nearly every day, with jam, of course; the apricot danishes, the richly flavoured ice-cream that I loved with strawberries (they're still fine to eat). Meat dishes with creamy sauces, fish and chips, in fact, anything with chips. A french stick with brie or camembert – it was these poor food choices that contributed to the development of my diabetes.

However, I soon learned that I did have options: I could carry on overeating and drinking, and living the sedentary life, or become leaner, fitter and healthier.

When you are diagnosed with diabetes the type of food and how much you eat, become more important. This sounds dramatic but it is true. In the early months, I was the slowest person in the shopping aisle because I read all the nutrition information panels on packaged food. I also met many other people who either had type 2 diabetes or knew someone with it. I realised I was not alone, and could make changes to improve my health.

Stress is the unseen element in diabetes. I relaxed more, knowing this would be good for my health.

One of the best things about the diagnosis was that I met a dietitian who explained food choices to me in great detail. More importantly, she emphasised portion control. Less food means less weight and less work for the pancreas. I cut back on fruit juices and drank more water.

The other important thing I'd like to pass on to you is that regular meals with carbohydrate spread evenly over the day help to control blood glucose levels. I followed the meal plan handed to me: three regular meals and two to three small snacks each day. (Note: snacks are not required by everyone – speak to your diabetes team.) I made sure my carbohydrate food choices were nutritious 'slow release' type and limited foods that were high in fat and high in sugar. One dietitian asked me to aim for five servings of vegetables a day (1 serving = 1 cup salad or ½ cup cooked vegetables). I still have not managed to do this but I try.

The second thing: I joined a gym and became fitter and less stressed than I had been in years. About six months into the 'new me' I flew to see my son and his wife, who did not recognise me at first, then they both stepped back in amazement at this healthy mum. That was a great moment. All the food in the world could not have given me that much satisfaction.

Lynn P. Bryan

Lynn Bryan, freelance writer

All about diabetes

What is diabetes? Diabetes is a condition in which the amount of glucose (sugar) in the blood is too high. This is because the pancreas does not make enough insulin or the insulin that it does produce is unable to do its job properly. Insulin is needed by the body to move glucose from the blood stream into the muscles and cells, to be used for energy.

There are two main types of diabetes

Type 1

Type 1 diabetes is an autoimmune disease where the body actually destroys the cells that produce insulin. So there is no insulin present. It represents 10 to 15 per cent of all cases of diabetes and normally occurs in children or young adults but can also occur in adults. While we don't know the exact cause of type 1 diabetes, it is thought that some people have a genetic predisposition for this condition and when exposed to a trigger, possibly a viral infection, the immune system then destroys the insulin-producing cells in the pancreas. Type 1 diabetes is not caused by lifestyle factors. People with type 1 diabetes require insulin injections several times a day for life.

Dealing with diabetes In this book we have set out to give advice on how to eat well, enjoy healthy foods and keep blood glucose levels managed. We encourage you to increase your physical activity. Current guidelines recommend that you exercise for at least 30 minutes every day. This includes a mixture of aerobic exercises such as walking and resistance exercises such as lifting weights. It is very important to discuss any increase or change to your exercise routine with your doctor or diabetes educator.

Type 2

Type 2 diabetes has various risk factors such as family history or lifestyle. It results in there not being enough insulin to meet the body's need or the insulin that is produced is no longer working efficiently to move glucose from your blood into your cells (known as insulin resistance). It represents 85 to 90 per cent of all cases of diabetes. Lifestyle factors such as unhealthy eating and lack of physical activity can contribute to the development of type 2 diabetes. Other risk factors include family history, large waist circumference ('apple' shape), being overweight, certain ethnic backgrounds and pre-diabetes. Pre-diabetes is a condition that occurs when the blood glucose level is higher than normal but not high enough to be diagnosed as diabetes.

Type 2 is the most common form of diabetes. While it usually affects adults, more young people, and even children, are being diagnosed all the time. Often symptoms of type 2 diabetes go unnoticed as the disease develops gradually. Symptoms may include blurred vision, skin infections, slow healing, tingling and numbness in the feet. Sometimes no symptoms are noticed at all. Persistent high blood glucose (sugar) levels in either type 1 or type 2 diabetes can damage the body's organs. This damage is referred to as diabetes-related complications.

Healthy eating along with an active lifestyle can assist in the prevention and management of type 2 diabetes. A healthier lifestyle will not only also help you to maintain a healthier body weight, it also helps manage cholesterol, blood pressure and blood glucose levels. If you are using insulin or medication to help control blood glucose levels you should discuss any dietary changes with your doctor, dietitian or diabetes educator to maintain a safe balance.

While these complications are serious and can be life threatening, with appropriate lifestyle changes and attention to blood glucose control, people with diabetes can substantially reduce the risk of developing these complications.

Vitamin D deficiency has recently been associated with the development of type 2 diabetes. The main source of vitamin D comes from exposure to sunlight. Foods containing vitamin D include oily fish (salmon, mackerel, sardines and herring), eggs, and fortified foods (such as margarine). It is unusual for people to obtain adequate levels of vitamin D through dietary sources alone. Your doctor can order a simple blood test to assess your vitamin D level. If you are deficient your doctor may recommend that you take vitamin D supplements.

High glucose levels can affect:

Vision Diabetic retinopathy is the leading cause of blindness in Australians aged under 60. The development of retinopathy is strongly related to the length of time diabetes has been present and the degree of blood glucose control. Regular checks and treatment can prevent blindness caused by retinopathy.

Kidney function Your kidneys help to clean your blood. They remove waste from the blood and pass it out of the body in the urine. Over time diabetes can cause damage to the kidneys which causes them to leak. You won't notice damage to your kidneys until it's quite advanced so it is important you have your kidney function checked yearly to pick up any problems. Your kidneys are also affected by high blood pressure so that should get checked at least every three months.

Circulation and sensation to the lower limbs Neuropathy or peripheral nerve disease and vascular damage may lead to lack of sensation, leg ulcers and serious foot problems from which lower limb amputation may result. Personal daily foot checks and thorough annual foot examinations conducted by your doctor or podiatrist will help to reduce your risk of lower limb complications.

Large blood vessels People with diabetes are at increased risk of heart disease and stroke associated with high blood glucose levels, high blood pressure and cholesterol. High glucose levels can also increase the risk of infection, delay wound healing and increase the risk of gum disease.

Healthy snacks

	The aim is to make meals that are full of flavour and colour and well-balanced for good health. If you enjoy a snack between meals, keep the snack small and select healthy options. Snacks are not required by everyone; speak to your dietitian.
FRUITS	1 medium apple or pear or half a mango or 2 plums or 1 peach or 1 large slice of watermelon or ½ a rockmelon. Strawberries, raspberries, blackberries, blueberries, passionfruit and unsweetened rhubarb are free foods (ie you can eat as much of them as you like).
VEGETABLES	Vegetable sticks: celery, carrot, snow peas, capsicum.
NUTS	30g unsalted nuts such as cashews, walnuts or almonds.
BREADS	1 regular slice raisin or multigrain toast.
CEREAL	½ cup high-fibre breakfast cereal with ½ cup low-fat milk.
DRINKS	1 skim café latte or 250ml of a low-fat flavoured milk or soy milk, or fruit smoothie.
CAKES	1 small pikelet or wholemeal crumpet or 1 small fruit or plain scone with 1 teaspoon jam.
SAVOURY	3 rice cakes or 4 high-fibre crispbread biscuits topped with cottage cheese, slice of tomato and chives; half an english muffin with 1 slice reduced-fat cheese and slice tomato, or 2 pitta bread triangles, or a small can of baked beans.
DAIRY	200g tub of low-fat yogurt.

Depression

Living with a chronic illness such as diabetes and coping with the varied management regimes, along with the threat of developing complications such as damage to the eyes (retinopathy), nerves (neuropathy) and kidneys (nephropathy) can be very stressful and may increase the risk of depression. This is why it is very important that people diagnosed with diabetes have someone they can confide in, such as a health professional, family member, friend or workmate.

Managing diabetes

Type 2 diabetes cannot be cured. It can however be managed by adopting a healthy lifestyle and taking tablets and/or insulin, as required. Genetics does play a part in determining a person's weight and the likelihood of developing type 2 diabetes. An unhealthy diet high in saturated fat, low in fibre (ie low in vegetables, fruit and wholegrain breads and cereals), high in kilojoules (from too much fat, sugar, alcohol and larger portion sizes) and low in physical activity increases our risk of developing diabetes and other health problems.

People with diabetes are encouraged to follow the same healthy eating principles as the general population.

This means, three evenly spread meals a day. Daily intake should consist of 4-5 servings of high-fibre breads and cereal foods, at least 5 servings of vegetables, 2-3 servings of fruit, 2-3 servings of low-fat dairy products (including milk, yogurt and cheese) 1-2 servings lean protein (including meat, poultry, fish, legumes and nuts) and small amounts of good (unsaturated) fats.

The above recommendations are based on the following serving sizes	
BREADS AND CEREALS	1 serving = 2 slices bread or 1 medium bread roll or 1 cup cooked rice/pasta/noodles or 1 cup cooked porridge or ½ cup untoasted muesli or 1 cup high-fibre cereal.
VEGETABLES	1 serving = 1 cup salad or 75g cooked vegetables/legumes or 1 small potato.
FRUIT	1 serving = 1 medium piece of fruit (150g) or 1 cup diced pieces or 1 cup drained canned fruit or ½ cup fruit juice.
DAIRY PRODUCTS	1 serving = 1 cup (250ml) milk or 1 small carton (200g) yogurt or 2 slices cheese.
LEAN PROTEIN	1 serving = 65-100g cooked meat or 80-120g cooked fish fillet or 2 small eggs or ½ cup legumes (eg beans, lentils, chickpeas) or ⅓ cup nuts.

Re-educate your palate away from the sweet and fatty food it has come to expect. It is a truism that you only have to taste a food 10 times for your palate to become accustomed to it.

Managing your lifestyle

Keep a record of your food intake, physical activity and blood glucose levels. This allows you to determine the impact of food, physical activity and your diabetes treatment (tablets and insulin) on your blood glucose levels (BGLs). If you find your BGLs are elevated 2 hours after a meal:

1. Have you eaten more carbohydrate than usual at your meal? If so, reduce the amount eaten next time and measure your BGL to determine the impact.
2. Consider swapping high GI carbohydrate foods for lower GI options (see the section on Low GI Foods)
3. Go for a walk.
4. Talk to your dietitian and diabetes team; if your blood glucose elevation is not lifestyle related you need to discuss with the team managing your diabetes about adjusting your diabetes treatment.

Note: elevated BGLs can be due to other reasons including illness or infection.

Free vegetables

Non-starchy vegetables or 'free vegetables' are virtually carbohydrate and kilojoule free. This means they have very little impact on your blood glucose levels and weight. You can eat as many free vegetables as you like. They include the following:

- artichoke
- asparagus
- beetroot
- broccoli
- brussels sprouts
- cabbage
- capsicum
- cauliflower
- celery
- cucumber
- eggplant
- green beans
- leek
- lettuce
- mushroom
- onion
- pumpkin
- radish
- salad greens
- spinach
- tomatoes
- zucchini

Carbohydrates

Carbohydrate foods are the best source of energy for the body. When carbohydrate foods are digested they break down to form glucose. If you eat regular meals and spread your carbohydrate foods evenly throughout the day, you will help maintain your energy levels without causing large rises in your blood glucose levels. Choose nutritious carbohydrate foods that are higher in fibre and lower in fat. Carbohydrate foods tend to be an excellent source of fibre, vitamins and minerals. Approximately half of all kilojoules (or calories) should come from carbohydrate foods.

Less nutritious forms of carbohydrate include chocolate, cakes, biscuits, pastries, lollies, regular ice-cream and soft drink. These foods are high in fat and sugar and are not suitable for everyday eating.

Carbohydrate foods include:

- Bread or bread rolls – choose wholegrain, wholemeal, rye, fruit bread.
- Breakfast cereals – choose high-fibre varieties such as rolled oats, bran cereals or untoasted muesli.
- Pasta, rice (basmati or doongara or brown) and other grains such as barley, burghul and couscous.
- Starchy vegetables – potatoes, sweet potato, yams, sweet corn, parsnip.
- Legumes – baked beans, kidney beans, chickpeas, lentils, three-bean mix.
- Fruit – all types such as apples, oranges, peaches, bananas, melons. Fruit is a good source of fibre.
- Milk products or dairy alternatives – choose low-fat varieties of milk, soy drink (calcium fortified), yogurt.
- High-fibre crispbreads.

As a protein and a carbohydrate, legumes are a tasty alternative to lean meat, poultry and fish as well as potato, pasta and rice.

Fat

Fats have the highest kilojoule (or calorie) content of all the nutrients. Eating too much fat may result in excess weight, which in the long run makes it more difficult to manage your blood glucose levels. A healthy eating plan, which is lower in fat, particularly saturated fat, is advised to help prevent and manage type 2 diabetes.

Saturated fat

It is important to limit saturated fat because it raises total and LDL (bad) cholesterol levels. Saturated fat is also linked with insulin resistance. Saturated fat is found in animal foods such as fatty meat, full-fat dairy products, butter and cheese. It is also found in palm oil (found in solid cooking fats, snack foods or convenience foods) and coconut products such as copha, coconut milk or cream. Not all fats are bad:
Some fat is important for good health. Mono and polyunsaturated fats do not raise cholesterol levels. Use a variety of polyunsaturated and monounsaturated fats to achieve a good balance. These include:
• Monounsaturated fats – sources include macadamias, avocados and olive oil.
• Polyunsaturated fats – sources include walnuts and oily fish which contain Omega-3, and seeds and seed oils, for example sesame and safflower, which contain Omega-6.
Almonds, cashews, hazelnuts, macadamias, peanuts, pecans and pistachios are higher in monounsaturated fats while brazil nuts, pine nuts and walnuts have more polyunsaturated fats. Walnuts are one of the few plant foods that contain the essential omega-3 fat, ALA, with smaller amounts also found in pecans, hazelnuts and macadamias.
Instead of frying, try steaming or grilling foods. You will be pleasantly surprised at how good steamed foods taste.
Fillo pastry is low in fat but not GI. Brush with skim milk instead of melted butter when preparing it.

Shopping advice

• Never shop for food when you are hungry.
• Make a shopping list and stick to it. This avoids the temptation to add chips and lollies to the trolley.
• Shop when you have plenty of time, so you can read the nutritional information on packages and you won't be tempted to make bad choices because you're in a hurry.
• Stick to the perimeter of the supermarket. This is where you find the fresh fruit, vegies, meat and dairy.
• As American author and food activist Michael Pollan advises: Don't buy anything your great-grandmother wouldn't recognise. This eliminates most over-processed foods and sticks to the foods nature provides.

Portion control The key to portion control is to downsize some foods and increase others to achieve a balanced plate. Teach yourself to judge the size of each portion with your eyes. Try to have lots of free vegetables and a balanced amount of protein and carbohydrate. Eating more free vegetables at meal times can help replace other high-kilojoule foods and fill you up.

Low GI foods:
• Fruit – apples, apricots, bananas, grapefruit, grapes, kiwi fruit, oranges, peach, pears, plums.
• Al dente pasta instead of most white potato varieties.
• legumes.
• sweet corn.
• peas.
• Add lentils, barley, split peas, haricot beans and pasta pieces to soups.
• Add kidney or borlotti beans or lentils to soups and casseroles.
• Add lentils, canned beans and even rolled oats to rissoles in combination with the meat base.
• Breakfast cereals. Use unprocessed rolled oats, oat brans, rice bran, lower-fat muesli.
• Ice-cream – look for low GI and low-fat varieties.
• Jam – look for 100 per cent fruit or low GI varieties and use without butter.
• Milk should be low fat or no fat.
• Pasta – all varieties are low GI, but wholemeal varieties are a better choice because they have a higher fibre, vitamin and mineral content.
• Vinegar and vinaigrette dressings can lower blood glucose levels by slowing the rate of food emptying from the stomach. Red or white wine vinegars are both good choices.
• Yogurt is best bought in the low-fat variety. No added sugar versions are better choices.

What is GI?

The more low GI (Glycemic Index) carbohydrates in the meal, the greater the health benefits. Why is GI important? Both the quantity and quality of the carbohydrate in a food counts. The GI is a measure of carbohydrate absorption/release. Low GI foods (GI less than or equal to 55) are those carbohydrate-containing foods that have a slow rate of digestion and absorption so they do not raise your blood glucose levels too rapidly. Therefore you should select mostly foods with a low GI for your main meals and snacks. An interesting note: the way a food is cooked can influence its GI rating. If the food is overcooked so that it is 'broken down' too much it will have a higher GI than it would in its less-processed state, eg: mashed potato has a higher GI than boiled or baked potato, and over-cooked rice or pasta will have a higher GI compared to when they are cooked al dente.

The GI values we have given for the recipes in this book are estimates only.

Low GI pantry staples

High quality wholegrain bread (around 20 kibbled grains) – whole or cracked grains; in baked goods, use oat bran, rice bran or rolled oats instead of flour if suitable for the recipe.

Rice – basmati, doongara, rather than jasmine or short-grain rice, or use pearl barley, buckwheat, bulgur, couscous. Be careful, it's not the colour of the rice that determines its GI value – brown basmati rice will have a low GI but other brown varieties probably won't.

Orange-fleshed sweet potato or kumara in preference to most varieties of white potato. Sweet potato is higher in fibre, which helps to slow the digestion and absorption of glucose into the blood. It is also lower in starch than most varieties of white potato and therefore has a lower GI value. Nicola, carisma and almera are varieties of white potato with GI values similar to orange-fleshed sweet potato. Most varieties of white potatoes have a high GI because they contain large amounts of easily digested starches that produce a rapid rise in blood glucose levels. Some varieties of new potatoes have lower levels because they have higher levels of harder-to-digest starch, but most are still considered moderate-to-high.

Eating out

This is one situation where you have minimal control on the size of the portion on your plate, and to a lesser extent, how the food is cooked. However, you can select each dish wisely.

• Pick the wholemeal roll.

• No butter.

• For an entrée, choose a salad-based dish, steamed vegetables or soup instead of anything deep-fried.

Be aware of your total carbohydrate intake and how it is prepared. Be cautious of chips or mashed potato, pasta, rice and breads prepared with butter, creamy sauces or cheese.

• Select a salad accompaniment, roasted or steamed vegetables without a cream-based sauce or butter. Ask if the chef will add ground black pepper and fresh lemon juice as a substitute.

• Some meals provide excess food. Consider asking for a smaller portion, or if you can order an entrée as a main course.

• Eating Italian? Avoid the heavy lasagnes and creamy pasta sauces. Instead, select a dish with fresh tomato sauce. The same criteria apply to dining in an Indian or classic French restaurant.

• When faced with a buffet, choose healthier foods over those you know aren't good for you. Try to keep in mind the limits of the carbohydrates for each serving.

• When dining at a friend's or even a relative's house, warn them beforehand that you have dietary requirements. It saves you the embarrassment of saying no to food they have created for your visit, and the host being mortified that they cannot serve you the best meal for your health.

• Desserts can be oh-so tempting. Fresh fruit and yogurt are good choices. A good restaurant will ask the chef to make it fresh for you.

• Drink: both men and women should not have more than two standard drinks a day. It is also recommended that you have some alcohol-free days each week.

Before going out

You can apply a few strategies to avoid overeating when you dine out. One is to drink a full glass of water before leaving home; another is to have a small snack such as a small cup of soup or a small plate of leafy green salad (ideally without any dressing) so that you are not that hungry when it is time to order.

About these recipes

We provide the kilojoule content so you can stay within recommended energy intake guidelines. Daily energy intake requirements vary among individuals according to your age, body weight, level of physical activity and whether you need to lose or gain weight.

Energy (kilojoules)
Average adults daily intake should be around 7500-8000 kilojoules.

Total fat
Daily intake should be limited to 30-35 per cent of total kilojoules; that is, 40-50g of fat per day.

Saturated fat
Fat intake should be less than seven per cent of total daily kilojoule allowance; that is, less than 10g daily.

Carbohydrates
Daily intake should be 50-60 per cent of total kilojoules; that is, 200-250g per day. Use low GI, high-fibre carbohydrate sources wherever possible.

Dietary fibre
Recommendations are 28g for women and 38g for men of dietary fibre daily.

Protein
Protein intake should be 10-15 per cent of total daily kilojoules. The ideal intake should be no more than 80-100g per day. As a guideline, allow 1g of protein for each kg of your ideal body weight; ie an 80kg person should eat only 80g of protein a day.

There is a lot of diet information available from your doctor and your dietitian as well as from the Australian Diabetes Council. Read all you can and make a plan that will help you deal with diabetes without changing your life too much.

portion control

Never pile food higher than a deck of cards.
Diameter of inside rim of plate is 20cm.

Lean protein
65-100g chicken breast
or fish fillet or lean steak

Free vegetables/salad
(eat as much as you like)
Lettuce, broccoli,
broccolini, asparagus,
celery, green beans,
beetroot, tomatoes,
cabbage, capsicum,
cauliflower, cucumber,
brussels sprouts,
mushrooms, onion,
leeks, spinach, squash,
leafy salad mixes,
zucchini, radish.

High-fibre/
Low GI carbohydrate
Steamed couscous,
pasta or rice (basmati
or doongara), or
wholegrain bread, or
mashed kumara or
1 corn on the cob

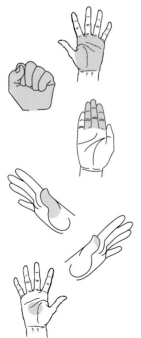

Visual reminder using your hand - per serving

palm of hand
• portion of cooked fish, skinless chicken or lean meat.

fist
• approximately 1 cup fresh fruit; 1 serving of low-fat milk or yogurt.

three middle fingers together
size of potato.

length of thumb
• amount of low-fat salad dressing.
• amount of avocado.

tip of thumb
• amount of unsaturated oil; amount of jam/vegemite/peanut butter.
• amount of unsaturated margarine.

centre of cupped palm (approximately 50c piece)
• amount of unsalted nuts; amount of reduced-fat cheese.

7-day menu planner

DAY	BREAKFAST	SNACK	LUNCH	SNACK	DINNER	DESSERT	TOTAL DAILY INTAKE
MONDAY	Porridge with banana and walnuts (page 19) plus 1 slice wholegrain bread	¼ cup unsalted nuts	Cheese and salad sandwich (page 37) plus a green salad	1 apple plus 1 small tub low-fat fruit yogurt	Fish and oven-roasted chips (page 101) plus a green salad	Cranberry macerated berries (page 106)	27.3g total fat (8.1g saturated fat); 4427kJ (1059 cal); 125.2g carbohydrate; 66.3g protein; 30g fibre
TUESDAY	Blueberry muffin (page 23) plus 1 small tub low-fat fruit yogurt	½ cup straw-berries	Butternut pumpkin soup (page 40) plus a green salad	1 pear	Thai basil chicken stir-fry (page 76)	Mango, berry and passionfruit frozen yogurt (page 108)	12.1g total fat (2.4g saturated fat); 4481kJ (1072 cal); 161.9g carbohydrate; 65.7g protein; 28g fibre
WEDNESDAY	Rolled barley fruit trifle (page 22) plus 1 slice toasted wholemeal bread with unsaturated margarine and Vegemite	1 banana	Chickpea salad (page 41)	1 small tub low-fat fruit yogurt	Seared tuna with chilled soba (page 94) plus a green salad	Tiramisu (page 113)	34g total fat (11.6g saturated fat); 4857kJ (1162 cal); 118g carbohydrate; 77.9g protein; 28.8g fibre
THURSDAY	Cheesy corn on rye (page 27)	1 small tub low-fat fruit yogurt	Tuna, celery and dill sandwich (page 36) plus a green salad	2 kiwi fruit	Chilli coriander lamb and barley salad (page 66)	Citrus salad (page 107)	20.8g total fat (6.6g saturated fat); 5140kJ (1230 cal); 159.4g carbohydrate; 84.4g protein; 34.2g fibre
FRIDAY	Bran and cranberry muesli (page 29)	½ cup blue-berries plus 1 small tub low-fat fruit yogurt	Chicken and vegetable rice paper rolls (page 42)	1 orange	Steaks with capsicum salsa (page 82) plus steamed beans and a green salad	Rosewater and raspberry jellies (page 110)	24.2g total fat (10.6g saturated fat); 4213kJ (1008 cal); 113.7g carbohydrate; 73g protein; 29.8g fibre
SATURDAY	Oven-baked rösti with breakfast beans (page 24)	1 small tub low-fat fruit yogurt	Asparagus frittata with rocket (page 55)	½ cup straw-berries	Herb stuffed chicken with tomato salad (page 65)	Vanilla ice-cream with mango and berry coulis (page 105)	20.5g total fat (4.6g saturated fat); 3787kJ (906 cal); 94.3g carbohydrate; 76.6g protein; 28.2g fibre
SUNDAY	Brekky berry smoothie (page 18)	½ cup straw-berries plus 1 small tub low-fat fruit yogurt	Carrot and lentil soup with caraway toasts (page 54) plus a green salad	¼ cup unsalted nuts	Linguine marinara (page 67) plus a green salad	Baked apples with berries (page 111) plus 1 small tub low-fat fruit yogurt	12.4g total fat (3.4g saturated fat); 4799kJ (1148 cal); 153.4g carbohydrate; 90.8g protein; 37.5g fibre

This menu planner is a guide only. It is important that you eat a balanced diet in order to get all the nutrients your body requires. See page 11 for daily recommended intakes.

breakfast

blueberry hotcakes

1 egg, separated
2 egg whites, extra
½ cup (125ml) apple sauce
1 teaspoon vanilla extract
3 cups (840g) low-fat yogurt
1¾ cups (280g) wholemeal self-raising flour
230g (7 ounces) fresh blueberries

1   Beat all egg whites in small bowl with electric mixer until soft peaks form.
2   Combine egg yolk, apple sauce, extract, 2 cups (560g) of the yogurt, flour and half the blueberries in large bowl; fold in egg whites, in two batches.

3   Heat oiled small frying pan; pour ¼ cup (60ml) of the batter into pan. Cook until bubbles appear on surface. Turn hotcake; cook until browned lightly. Remove from pan; cover to keep warm. Repeat with remaining batter.
4   Serve hotcakes topped with remaining yogurt and blueberries.

prep + cook time 35 minutes **serves** 6
nutritional count per serving 2.3g total fat (0.7g saturated fat); 1233kJ (295 cal); 46.2g carbohydrate; 17.5g protein; 6.2g fibre; 455mg sodium; low GI

Blueberries, with a juicy centre and sweet taste, have easily become one of our year-round, all-time-favourite berries.

46.2g Carb

15

smoked salmon and poached egg on rye

4 eggs
170g (5½ ounces) asparagus, halved crossways
4 slices (180g) rye bread, toasted
200g (6½ ounces) smoked salmon
2 tablespoons fresh chervil leaves

1 Half fill large shallow frying pan with water; bring to the boil. Break eggs into cup, one at a time, then slide into pan. When all eggs are in pan, allow water to return to a boil.

2 Cover pan, turn off heat; stand about 4 minutes or until a light film sets over egg yolks. Remove eggs, one at a time, using slotted spoon; place spoon on absorbent-paper-lined saucer briefly to blot up poaching liquid.

3 Meanwhile, boil, steam or microwave asparagus until tender; drain.

4 Divide toast among serving plates; top each with salmon, asparagus then egg. Serve sprinkled with chervil.

prep + cook time 15 minutes **serves** 4
nutritional count per serving 8.8g total fat
(2.2g saturated fat); 1175kJ (281 cal);
24.5g carbohydrate; 23.7g protein;
4.1g fibre; 1164mg sodium; low GI

24.5g Carbs

brekky berry smoothie

½ cup (75g) frozen mixed berries
½ cup (125ml) chilled low-fat milk
¼ cup (70g) low-fat vanilla-flavoured yogurt
1 weet-bix (15g), crushed

1 Blend ingredients until smooth.
2 Pour into glass; serve immediately.

prep time 5 minutes **makes** 1 cup (250ml)
nutritional count per serving 0.8g total fat
(0.2g saturated fat); 765kJ (183 cal);
28.7g carbohydrate; 13.1g protein;
3.3g fibre; 177mg sodium; low GI

mango lassi

1 medium ripe mango (430g), peeled,
  chopped coarsely
1 cup (250ml) buttermilk
⅓ cup (95g) low-fat fruit-flavoured yogurt
2 tablespoons lime juice

1 Blend ingredients until smooth.
2 Pour into glasses; serve immediately.

prep time 10 minutes **serves** 2
nutritional count per serving 3g total fat
(1.7g saturated fat); 849kJ (203 cal);
32.6g carbohydrate; 9.6g protein;
2.3g fibre; 105mg sodium; low GI

28.7g

32.6g

porridge with banana and walnuts

2 cups (500ml) water
1 cup (250ml) low-fat milk
1⅓ cups (120g) rolled oats
2 medium bananas (400g), sliced thickly
½ cup (50g) walnuts, chopped coarsely
1 tablespoon honey
1⅓ cups (330ml) low-fat milk, extra

1 Combine the water and milk in medium saucepan; bring to the boil. Reduce heat; add oats. Simmer, stirring, about 5 minutes or until porridge is thick and creamy.
2 Serve porridge topped with banana, nuts, honey and extra milk.

prep + cook time 15 minutes **serves** 4
nutritional count per serving 14.2g total fat (4.4g saturated fat); 1517kJ (363 cal); 44.9g carbohydrate; 12.3g protein; 5.5g fibre; 92mg sodium; low GI

bircher muesli with figs and pistachios

1½ cups (135g) rolled oats
¼ cup (30g) oat bran
¼ cup (15g) natural bran flakes
¾ cup (180ml) low-fat milk
¾ cup (180ml) orange juice
¾ cup (200g) low-fat greek-style yogurt
½ teaspoon ground cinnamon
½ cup (70g) roasted pistachios, chopped coarsely
1 large orange (300g), segmented
2 medium fresh figs (120g), sliced thinly

1 Combine cereals, milk, juice, yogurt and cinnamon in large bowl. Cover, refrigerate overnight. Stir in half the nuts.
2 Divide muesli among serving bowls; top with orange segments, figs and remaining nuts.

prep time 15 minutes (+ refrigeration) **serves** 4
nutritional count per serving 16.9g total fat (4.4g saturated fat); 1726kJ (413 cal); 46.8g carbohydrate; 14.4g protein; 8.4g fibre; 98mg sodium; low GI

44.9g Carbs

46.8g

cheese and herb egg-white omelette

12 egg whites
4 green onions (scallions), sliced thinly
¼ cup finely chopped fresh chives
¼ cup finely chopped fresh chervil
½ cup finely chopped fresh flat-leaf parsley
⅓ cup (40g) coarsely grated reduced-fat
  cheddar cheese
⅓ cup (35g) coarsely grated reduced-fat
  mozzarella cheese
4 slices (180g) soy-linseed bread, toasted

1 Preheat grill (broiler).
2 Beat a quarter of the egg whites in small bowl with electric mixer until soft peaks form; fold in a quarter of the combined onion and herbs.
3 Pour mixture into 20cm (8-inch) heated lightly oiled non-stick frying pan; cook, uncovered, over low heat until omelette is browned lightly underneath.
4 Sprinkle a quarter of the combined cheeses on half of the omelette. Place pan under preheated grill (broiler) until cheese begins to melt and omelette sets; fold omelette over to completely cover cheese. Carefully slide onto serving plate; cover to keep warm.
5 Repeat process three times with remaining egg white, onion and herb mixture, and cheese. Serve omelettes with toast and extra chopped herbs.

prep + cook time 35 minutes **serves** 4
nutritional count per serving 3g total fat (1.5g saturated fat); 823kJ (197 cal); 18.7g carbohydrate; 21.5g protein; 4g fibre; 389mg sodium; low GI

18.7g Carb

LSA is a mixture of ground linseeds, sunflower seed kernels and almonds; available in health-food shops or the health-food section in supermarkets.

rolled barley fruit trifle

250g (8 ounces) strawberries, quartered
1 medium mango (430g), chopped coarsely
2 cups (560g) low-fat yogurt
½ cup (60g) rolled barley
⅓ cup (40g) LSA
1 tablespoon honey

1 Combine strawberries and mango in small bowl.
2 Divide half the fruit between four 1½-cup (375ml) glasses. Top with half the yogurt. Divide barley, LSA, honey and remaining yogurt among glasses.
3 Cover glasses and remaining fruit separately; refrigerate overnight.
4 Top trifles with remaining fruit to serve.

prep time 15 minutes (+ refrigeration) **serves** 4
nutritional count per serving 6.2g total fat (0.7g saturated fat); 1104kJ (264 cal); 32.6g carbohydrate; 14.8g protein; 6.8g fibre; 133mg sodium; low GI

blueberry muffins

1 cup (150g) white self-raising flour
1 cup (160g) wholemeal self-raising flour
½ cup (110g) firmly packed light brown sugar
2 egg whites, beaten lightly
⅓ cup (80ml) apple sauce
¾ cup (180ml) low-fat milk
150g (4½ ounces) fresh or frozen blueberries

1 Preheat oven to 180°C/350°F. Grease 12-hole
(⅓-cup/80ml) muffin pan.
2 Sift flours into large bowl; stir in sugar.
3 Stir in combined egg whites, apple sauce and
milk. Do not over-mix; mixture should be lumpy.
Add berries; stir through gently.
4 Spoon mixture into pan holes. Bake about
20 minutes. Stand 5 minutes before turning, top-
side up, onto wire rack to cool.

prep + cook time 35 minutes (+ standing) **makes** 12
nutritional count per muffin 0.5g total fat
(0.1g saturated fat); 602kJ (144 cal);
29.8g carbohydrate; 4.3g protein;
2.3g fibre; 195mg sodium; medium GI

Store muffins in an airtight container for up
to two days, or freeze for up to one month.

oven-baked rösti with breakfast beans

1 small kumara (orange sweet potato) (250g),
  grated coarsely
1 medium potato (200g), grated coarsely
1 teaspoon coarse cooking (kosher) salt
1 egg
2 tablespoons wholemeal self-raising flour
1 small red onion (100g), chopped finely
2 teaspoons olive oil

BREAKFAST BEANS
2 teaspoons olive oil
1 medium brown onion (150g), sliced thinly
2 cloves garlic, crushed
410g (13 ounces) can diced tomatoes
¼ cup (60ml) water
400g (12½ ounces) can cannellini beans,
  rinsed, drained
¼ cup coarsely chopped fresh flat-leaf parsley

1 Make breakfast beans.
2 Preheat oven to 200°C/400°F.
3 Combine kumara, potato and salt in medium bowl; stand 5 minutes then squeeze out liquid.
4 Whisk egg in medium bowl; whisk in flour. Stir in onion and kumara mixture.
5 Heat oil in large ovenproof frying pan over medium heat; add kumara mixture, press down firmly. Cook rösti about 3 minutes or until browned lightly underneath. Transfer pan to oven; bake, uncovered, about 20 minutes or until browned. Turn rösti onto chopping board, cut into eight wedges; serve with breakfast beans.

BREAKFAST BEANS Heat oil in medium saucepan, add onion and garlic; cook, stirring, until onion softens. Stir in undrained tomatoes, the water and beans; bring to the boil. Reduce heat; simmer, uncovered, about 10 minutes or until thick. Remove from heat; stir in parsley.

prep + cook time 40 minutes (+ standing) serves 4
nutritional count per serving 6.5g total fat
(1.1g saturated fat); 836kJ (200 cal);
24.5g carbohydrate; 7.7g protein;
6g fibre; 138mg sodium; medium GI

Cannellini beans are amazingly good for you. They are loaded with nutrients including iron, magnesium and folate, and are an excellent source of fibre.
If your frying pan handle is not ovenproof, wrap it well in foil to protect it in the oven. We used a frying pan with a base measuring 22cm (9 inches).

breakfast fry up

4 medium egg (plum) tomatoes (300g), quartered
2 tablespoons balsamic vinegar
cooking-oil spray
300g (9½ ounces) button mushrooms,
  sliced thickly
½ cup loosely packed fresh basil leaves
¼ cup coarsely chopped fresh flat-leaf parsley
4 eggs
200g (6½ ounces) shaved salt-reduced lean ham
8 slices (360g) soy-linseed bread, toasted

1 Preheat oven to 200°C/400°F.
2 Combine tomato and half the vinegar in medium shallow baking dish; spray lightly with cooking-oil spray. Roast about 20 minutes.
3 Meanwhile, cook mushrooms and remaining vinegar in medium oiled frying pan until tender; stir in herbs. Transfer to serving dishes; cover to keep warm.
4 Fry eggs in same cleaned heated oiled frying pan until cooked as you like. Remove eggs from pan. Heat ham in same pan. Serve eggs, ham, mushrooms and tomato with toast.

prep + cook time 35 minutes serves 4
nutritional count per serving 9.7g total fat (2.6g saturated fat); 1568kJ (375 cal); 30.7g carbohydrate; 28.3g protein; 9.4g fibre; 444mg sodium; low GI

cheesy corn on rye

310g (10 ounces) canned corn kernels,
  rinsed, drained
2 tablespoons low-fat ricotta cheese
40g (1½ ounces) baby spinach leaves
2 slices rye bread (90g), toasted

1 Heat corn in medium heatproof bowl in
microwave oven on HIGH (100%) for about
30 seconds; stir in cheese and spinach.
2 Serve toast topped with corn mixture.

prep + cook time 5 minutes **serves** 2
nutritional count per serving 4.4g total fat
(1.7g saturated fat); 1120kJ (268 cal);
42.2g carbohydrate; 10.6g protein;
7.2g fibre; 595mg sodium; low GI

42.2g Carbs

27

scrambled eggs florentine

4 eggs
6 egg whites
2 tablespoons low-fat milk
2 tablespoons finely chopped fresh chives
2 teaspoons olive oil
150g (4½ ounces) baby spinach leaves
8 slices (360g) soy-linseed bread, toasted

1 Whisk eggs, egg whites, milk and chives in
medium bowl. Heat oil in large frying pan, add egg
mixture; cook, stirring, over low heat until creamy.
2 Place spinach in colander over sink; pour over
about 2 cups of boiling water. Drain well.
3 Serve spinach and eggs with toast.

prep + cook time 20 minutes serves 4
nutritional count per serving 13g total fat
(2.7g saturated fat); 1463kJ (350 cal);
29.2g carbohydrate; 25.6g protein;
7.4g fibre; 572mg sodium; low GI

bran and cranberry muesli

1 cup (90g) rolled oats
¾ cup (55g) all-bran
¼ cup (35g) dried cranberries
2 cups (500ml) low-fat milk
1 large banana (230g), sliced thinly
125g (4 ounces) fresh raspberries

1 Combine oats, bran and cranberries in small bowl to make muesli mixture.
2 Place ⅓ cup muesli in each bowl; top with milk, banana and raspberries.

prep time 10 minutes **serves** 6
nutritional count per serving 2.1g total fat
(0.4g saturated fat); 723kJ (173 cal);
28.3g carbohydrate; 7.6g protein;
6.2g fibre; 122mg sodium; low GI

If you don't want to use dried cranberries, use sultanas or raisins.

berry buckwheat pancakes

1 cup (160g) wholemeal self-raising flour
½ cup (75g) buckwheat flour
1 tablespoon caster (superfine) sugar
½ teaspoon ground cinnamon
2 eggs, beaten lightly
1⅓ cups (330ml) low-fat milk
1 cup (150g) frozen mixed berries, thawed
2 tablespoons orange juice
1 tablespoon icing (confectioners') sugar
⅔ cup (160g) low-fat yogurt

1 Combine flours, caster sugar and cinnamon in medium bowl; gradually whisk in combined eggs and milk until batter is smooth. Cover, refrigerate 30 minutes.
2 Meanwhile, blend or process berries, juice and icing sugar until pureed.
3 Pour ⅓ cup (80ml) batter into heated oiled medium frying pan. Spoon 1 level teaspoon of berry puree on top of pancake batter; using skewer, gently swirl puree through batter to marble. Cook pancake until bubbles appear on surface. Turn pancake; cook until browned lightly. Remove from pan; cover to keep warm.
4 Repeat process, using ⅓ cup (80ml) batter and 1 teaspoon puree for each pancake, to make a total of eight pancakes.
5 Serve pancakes with the remaining berry puree and yogurt.

prep + cook time 25 minutes (+ refrigeration)
serves 4
nutritional count per serving 4.3g total fat
(1.2 g saturated fat); 1501kJ (359 cal);
59.3g carbohydrate; 17.6g protein;
5.9g fibre; 387mg sodium; medium GI

serving suggestion Serve with fresh berries.

Buckwheat flour is available in health-food shops or the health-food section in supermarkets.

59.3g Carbs

lunches and
light meals

tomato and kumara brown rice salad

1 cup (200g) brown long-grain rice
1 small kumara (orange sweet potato) (250g),
   chopped coarsely
250g (8 ounces) red grape tomatoes, halved
2 green onions (scallions), sliced thinly
⅓ cup firmly packed fresh small basil leaves
40g (1½ ounces) trimmed rocket leaves (arugula)

BALSAMIC DRESSING
2 tablespoons orange juice
1 tablespoon balsamic vinegar
1 teaspoon olive oil
1 clove garlic, crushed

1 Cook rice in large saucepan of boiling water,
uncovered, about 30 minutes or until tender; drain.
Rinse under cold water; drain.
2 Meanwhile, boil, steam or microwave kumara
until tender; drain.
3 Make balsamic dressing.
4 Combine rice, kumara and dressing in large
bowl with tomato, onion, basil and rocket.

BALSAMIC DRESSING Combine ingredients in
screw-top jar; shake well.

prep + cook time 40 minutes serves 4
nutritional count per serving 3g total fat
(0.5g saturated fat); 1287kJ (308 cal);
60.3g carbohydrate; 6.9g protein;
5g fibre; 18mg sodium; medium GI

vegetable burgers

2 teaspoons olive oil
1 large brown onion (200g), chopped finely
300g (9½ ounces) button mushrooms,
  chopped coarsely
1 medium red capsicum (bell pepper) (200g),
  chopped finely
1 clove garlic, crushed
1 cup (200g) red lentils
1 cup (250ml) salt-reduced vegetable stock
1 cup (250ml) water
1½ cups (250g) cooked brown long-grain rice
2 tablespoons finely chopped fresh
  flat-leaf parsley
⅓ cup (50g) plain (all-purpose) flour
2 medium carrots (240g), grated coarsely
200g (6½ ounces) low-fat greek-style yogurt
1 tablespoon finely chopped fresh mint
225g (7 ounces) canned sliced beetroot
  (beets), drained
1½ cups (60g) alfalfa sprouts
2 medium tomatoes (300g), sliced thinly
6 small wholemeal bread rolls, split, toasted

1 Heat oil in large frying pan, add onion, mushrooms, capsicum, garlic and lentils; cook, stirring, until vegetables soften. Add stock and the water; bring to the boil. Reduce heat; simmer, uncovered, stirring occasionally, about 10 minutes or until lentils are tender and stock is absorbed. Remove from heat. Stir in rice, parsley, flour and half of the carrot.
2 When cool enough to handle, shape mixture into six patties; place on baking-paper-lined tray. Cover; refrigerate 2 hours or until firm.
3 Cook patties in same cleaned, heated oiled frying pan until browned both sides and heated through.
4 Meanwhile, combine yogurt and mint in small bowl.
5 Sandwich patties, remaining carrot, beetroot, alfalfa, tomato and yogurt mixture between toasted roll halves.

prep + cook time 1 hour (+ refrigeration) serves 6
nutritional count per serving 3.6g total fat
(0.6g saturated fat); 1501kJ (359 cal);
56.8g carbohydrate; 18.9g protein;
11.9g fibre; 311mg sodium; medium GI

You need to cook ½ cup (100g) brown long-grain rice for this recipe.

56.8g Carbs

tuna, celery and dill sandwich

185g (6 ounces) canned tuna in springwater, drained, flaked
2 trimmed celery stalks (200g), chopped finely
¼ small red onion (25g), chopped finely
2 tablespoons low-fat ricotta cheese
1 tablespoon coarsely chopped fresh dill
2 teaspoons rinsed, drained baby capers
20g (¾ ounce) baby spinach leaves
4 slices (180g) rye bread, toasted

1 Combine tuna, celery, onion, cheese, dill and capers in medium bowl.
2 Sandwich spinach and tuna mixture between bread slices.

prep time 10 minutes makes 2
nutritional count per sandwich 6g total fat
(2.2g saturated fat); 1517kJ (363 cal);
42.5g carbohydrate; 29.9g protein;
8.4g fibre; 677mg sodium; medium GI

tip If you're taking this sandwich to work, make the filling the night before. Put it in the fridge when you arrive at work. Toast the bread and assemble the sandwich at work.

cheese and salad sandwich

200g (6½ ounces) low-fat cottage cheese
⅓ cup (40g) coarsely grated reduced-fat
  cheddar cheese
½ cup shredded baby spinach leaves
130g (4 ounces) canned corn kernels, rinsed, drained
1 green onion (scallion), sliced thinly
1 small carrot (70g), finely grated
1 tablespoon sesame seeds, roasted
2 teaspoons lemon juice
30g (1 ounce) mesclun
8 slices (360g) wholemeal bread

1 Combine cheeses, spinach, corn, onion, carrot, seeds and juice in medium bowl.
2 Sandwich mesclun and cheese mixture between bread slices.

prep time 15 minutes makes 4
nutritional count per sandwich 5.8g total fat
(1.4g saturated fat); 1350kJ (323 cal);
40.8g carbohydrate; 22.6g protein;
7.5g fibre; 644mg sodium; medium GI

chicken teriyaki brown rice sushi

1 cup (200g) brown short-grain rice
2 cups (500ml) water
1 tablespoon rice vinegar
3 sheets toasted nori (yaki-nori)
1 lebanese cucumber (130g), seeded, cut
  into matchsticks
20g (¾ ounce) snow pea sprouts, trimmed
2 tablespoons salt-reduced soy sauce

SUSHI VINEGAR
1 tablespoon rice vinegar
2 teaspoons white sugar
¼ teaspoon fine salt

CHICKEN TERIYAKI
120g (4 ounces) chicken breast fillet, sliced thinly
1 tablespoon teriyaki sauce
1 clove garlic, crushed

1 Wash rice in large bowl with cold water until water is almost clear. Drain rice in strainer for at least 30 minutes.
2 Meanwhile, make sushi vinegar and chicken teriyaki.
3 Place rice and the water in medium saucepan, cover tightly; bring to the boil. Reduce heat; simmer, covered, about 30 minutes or until water is absorbed. Remove from heat; stand, covered, 10 minutes.
4 Spread rice into a large, non-metallic, flat-bottomed bowl (a wooden bowl is good for this). Using plastic spatula, repeatedly slice through rice at a sharp angle to break up lumps and separate grains, gradually pouring in sushi vinegar at the same time.

5 Continue to slice and turn the rice mixture with one hand; fan the rice with the other hand about 5 minutes or until it is almost cool. Cover rice with damp cloth to stop it drying out while making sushi.
6 Add rice vinegar to medium bowl of cold water. Place one nori sheet, shiny-side down, lengthways across bamboo mat about 2cm (¾-inch) from edge of mat closest to you. Dip fingers of one hand into bowl of vinegared water, shake off excess; pick up a third of the rice, place across centre of nori sheet.
7 Wet fingers again, then, working from left to right, gently rake rice evenly over nori, leaving 2cm (¾-inch) strip on far side of nori uncovered. Build up rice in front of uncovered strip to form a mound to keep filling in place.
8 Place one-third of the cucumber, sprouts and chicken in a row across centre of rice, making sure the filling extends to both ends of the rice.
9 Starting with edge closest to you, pick up mat using thumb and index fingers of both hands; use remaining fingers to hold filling in place as you roll mat away from you. Roll forward, pressing gently but tightly, wrapping nori around rice and filling.
10 Working quickly, repeat process to make a total of three rolls. Cut each roll into four pieces. Serve with sauce and wasabi, if you like.

SUSHI VINEGAR Combine ingredients in small jug.

CHICKEN TERIYAKI Combine chicken, sauce and garlic in small bowl. Cook chicken mixture in heated oiled small frying pan, stirring, until cooked through. Cool.

prep + cook time 1 hour 20 minutes (+ cooling)
serves 4
nutritional count per serving 2.3g total fat
(0.5g saturated fat); 1058kJ (253 cal);
43.1g carbohydrate; 12.8g protein;
3.4g fibre; 551mg sodium; medium GI

butternut pumpkin soup

1 teaspoon olive oil
1 small leek (200g), sliced thinly
1 clove garlic, crushed
1 teaspoon ground cumin
½ teaspoon ground coriander
1kg (2 pounds) butternut pumpkin,
  chopped coarsely
1 large potato (300g), chopped coarsely
1 cup (250ml) salt-reduced chicken stock
3 cups (750ml) water
2 teaspoons fresh thyme leaves
8 slices (360g) soy-linseed bread, toasted

1 Heat oil in large saucepan; cook leek and garlic, stirring, until leek is tender. Add spices; cook, stirring, until fragrant.
2 Add pumpkin, potato, stock and the water to pan; bring to the boil. Reduce heat; simmer, covered, about 20 minutes or until the vegetables are tender. Cool 10 minutes.
3 Blend or process mixture, in batches, until smooth. Return mixture to pan; stir until hot. Sprinkle soup with thyme; serve with toast.

prep + cook time 35 minutes **serves** 4
nutritional count per serving 4.4g total fat
(0.7g saturated fat); 1559kJ (373 cal);
59.6g carbohydrate; 16.6g protein;
11.5g fibre; 377mg sodium; low GI

chickpea salad

125g (4 ounces) canned chickpeas (garbanzos),
  rinsed, drained
1 lebanese cucumber (130g), chopped coarsely
½ small red onion (50g), sliced thinly
¼ cup (40g) seeded kalamata olives
⅓ cup coarsely chopped fresh flat-leaf parsley
½ small yellow capsicum (bell pepper) (75g),
  chopped coarsely
1 small egg (plum) tomato (60g), seeded,
  chopped coarsely
2 tablespoons low-fat tzatziki
1 slice (45g) wholemeal bread, toasted

LEMON DRESSING
¼ teaspoon finely grated lemon rind
1 tablespoon lemon juice
1 teaspoon olive oil
¼ teaspoon ground cumin

1 Make lemon dressing.
2 Combine chickpeas, cucumber, onion, olives,
parsley, capsicum, tomato and lemon dressing in
medium bowl.
3 Serve the salad topped with tzatziki. Serve
with toast.

LEMON DRESSING Combine ingredients in small
bowl or jar.

prep time 15 minutes serves 1
nutritional count per serving 9.8g total fat
(2.4g saturated fat); 1530kJ (366 cal);
47.2g carbohydrate; 16.2g protein;
13g fibre; 823mg sodium; medium GI

You need one large bunch of fresh mint and another of fresh coriander for this recipe.

chicken and vegetable rice paper rolls

1 litre (4 cups) water
5cm (2-inch) piece fresh ginger (25g), sliced thinly
400g (12½ ounces) chicken breast fillets
150g (4½ ounces) bean thread noodles
1 teaspoon sesame oil
1 tablespoon lime juice
2 tablespoons sweet chilli sauce
24 x 21cm (8.5-inch) rice paper rounds
48 large fresh mint leaves
48 fresh coriander (cilantro) sprigs
2 medium carrots (240g), grated coarsely
2 medium red capsicums (bell peppers) (400g),
  sliced thinly
2 medium yellow capsicums (bell peppers) (400g),
  sliced thinly
150g (4½ ounces) snow peas, sliced thinly

COCONUT DIPPING SAUCE
1 teaspoon sesame oil
2 cloves garlic, crushed
2 green onions (scallions), sliced thinly
2 teaspoons finely grated fresh ginger
1½ cups (375ml) light coconut milk
1 teaspoon fish sauce
2 tablespoons lime juice
1 tablespoon sweet chilli sauce

1 Place the water and ginger in medium saucepan; bring to the boil. Add chicken, reduce heat; simmer gently, uncovered, about 10 minutes or until chicken is cooked through. Remove from heat; stand 10 minutes. Remove chicken with slotted spoon; discard liquid. When cool, slice chicken thinly. Cover, refrigerate 1 hour.
2 Meanwhile, make coconut dipping sauce.
3 Place noodles in large heatproof bowl, cover with boiling water; stand until tender, drain. Combine noodles in same bowl with oil, juice and sauce.
4 Dip one rice paper round into bowl of warm water until soft; place on board covered with clean tea-towel. Place 2 mint leaves and 2 coriander sprigs in centre of rice paper; top with a little of the carrot, capsicum, snow peas, noodles and sliced chicken. Fold and roll to enclose filling. Repeat with remaining ingredients to make a total of 24 rolls. Serve rolls with coconut dipping sauce.

COCONUT DIPPING SAUCE Heat oil in small saucepan, add garlic, onion and ginger; cook, stirring, until fragrant. Add coconut milk; bring to the boil. Reduce heat; simmer, uncovered, about 5 minutes or until thickened slightly. Strain mixture through fine sieve into small bowl; discard solids. Stir in fish sauce, juice and sweet chilli sauce; cool.

prep + cook time 1 hour 15 minutes (+ refrigeration)
serves 6
nutritional count per serving 8.7g total fat
(4.8g saturated fat); 1430kJ (342 cal);
39.8g carbohydrate; 22.6g protein;
5.5g fibre; 362mg sodium; medium GI

felafel rolls with tabbouleh

250g (8 ounces) frozen broad beans
250g (8 ounces) canned chickpeas (garbanzos), rinsed, drained
2 cloves garlic, crushed
6 green onions (scallions), chopped coarsely
1 teaspoon ground cumin
½ teaspoon ground coriander
¼ cup coarsely chopped fresh flat-leaf parsley
¼ cup coarsely chopped fresh mint
2 tablespoons polenta, approximately
cooking-oil spray
1 lebanese cucumber (130g)
1 baby cos lettuce (180g), leaves separated
4 large wholemeal pitta breads (320g)

TABBOULEH
2 tablespoons burghul
⅔ cup finely chopped fresh flat-leaf parsley
2 green onions (scallions), chopped finely
1 medium tomato (150g), chopped finely
2 teaspoons olive oil
1 teaspoon lemon juice

YOGURT SAUCE
⅔ cup (190g) low-fat yogurt
1 clove garlic, crushed
2 teaspoons lemon juice
2 teaspoons finely chopped fresh mint

1 Preheat oven to 220°C/425°F.
2 Place beans in medium heatproof bowl, cover with boiling water; stand 5 minutes, drain. Remove and discard skins.
3 Process beans, chickpeas, garlic, onion, spices and herbs until combined. Shape level tablespoons of mixture into patties; roll patties in polenta, place on oiled oven tray. Spray patties lightly with cooking-oil spray. Bake about 40 minutes.
4 Meanwhile, make tabbouleh and yogurt sauce.
5 Using a vegetable peeler, cut cucumber into ribbons lengthways. Divide lettuce, cucumber, felafel, tabbouleh and yogurt sauce among breads; roll up to enclose filling.

TABBOULEH Place burghul in small heatproof bowl, cover with boiling water; stand 10 minutes, drain. Pat dry with absorbent paper. Combine burghul with remaining ingredients in medium bowl.

YOGURT SAUCE Combine ingredients in small bowl.

prep + cook time 1 hour 15 minutes serves 4
nutritional count per serving 6.3g total fat (1g saturated fat); 1735kJ (415 cal); 62.3g carbohydrate; 18.9g protein; 15.2g fibre; 572mg sodium; low GI

spinach and cheese quesadillas

⅔ cup (130g) low-fat cottage cheese
100g (3 ounces) baby spinach leaves
1 medium avocado (230g), chopped finely
1 cup (200g) canned mexican-style beans, drained
310g (10 ounces) canned corn kernels, drained
2 medium tomatoes (300g), seeded, chopped finely
1 small red onion (100g), chopped finely
2 medium zucchini (240g), grated coarsely
16 x 15cm (6-inch) flour tortillas
1 cup (100g) coarsely grated reduced-fat
  mozzarella cheese
¼ cup loosely packed fresh coriander
  (cilantro) leaves

1 Blend or process cottage cheese and spinach
until smooth.
2 Combine avocado, beans, corn, tomato, onion
and zucchini in medium bowl.
3 Preheat grill (broiler).
4 Place eight tortillas on oven trays; spread
spinach mixture over tortillas, leaving 2cm (¾-inch)
border around edge. Spread avocado mixture over
spinach mixture; top each with the remaining tortillas.
5 Sprinkle mozzarella over quesadilla stacks. Cook
quesadillas under grill until browned lightly. Serve
sprinkled with coriander.

prep + cook time 40 minutes **serves** 8
nutritional count per serving 10.4g total fat
(3.2g saturated fat); 1170kJ (280 cal);
30.5g carbohydrate; 13.9g protein;
5.2g fibre; 465mg sodium; low GI

serving suggestion Serve with grated cabbage
and carrot salad tossed in a lime juice and fresh
coriander dressing.

Quesadillas are filled tortillas which are grilled or fried and served
with fresh salsa. They are best made and eaten as soon as they are
cool enough to handle.

30.5g Carbs

hummus

2 large wholemeal pitta bread (160g)
1 tablespoon lemon juice
½ small brown onion (40g), chopped finely
1 clove garlic, crushed
½ teaspoon ground cumin
200g (6½ ounces) canned chickpeas (garbanzos),
  rinsed, drained
¼ cup (60ml) low-fat milk
¼ teaspoon sesame oil
2 teaspoons finely chopped fresh
  coriander (cilantro)

1 Preheat oven to 180°C/350°F.
2 Cut bread into thin triangles; place on oven tray.
Bake about 8 minutes or until crisp.
3 Meanwhile, combine juice, onion and garlic in
small frying pan; cook, stirring, until onion softens.
4 Blend or process onion mixture with cumin,
chickpeas, milk and oil until smooth; stir in
coriander. Serve hummus with the pitta crisps.

prep + cook time 15 minutes serves 4
nutritional count per serving 1.9g total fat
(0.4g saturated fat); 640kJ (153 cal);
25.3g carbohydrate; 6.5g protein;
4.4g fibre; 284mg sodium; low GI

salmon pasta salad

1 cup (150g) spiral pasta
170g (5½ ounces) asparagus, trimmed,
   chopped coarsely
1 teaspoon finely grated lemon rind
¼ cup (60ml) lemon juice
1 clove garlic, crushed
2 tablespoons low-fat ricotta cheese
1 small red capsicum (bell pepper) (150g),
   sliced thinly
⅓ cup coarsely chopped fresh flat-leaf parsley
2 green onions (scallions), sliced thinly
210g (6½ ounces) canned pink salmon in
   springwater, drained, flaked

1 Cook pasta in medium saucepan of boiling
water, uncovered, until tender. Add asparagus;
cook 1 minute. Drain.
2 Meanwhile, combine rind, juice and garlic in
large bowl; add pasta, asparagus and remaining
ingredients to bowl; toss to combine.

prep + cook time 25 minutes **serves** 2
nutritional count per serving 8.5g total fat
(2.9g saturated fat); 1860kJ (445 cal);
56.4g carbohydrate; 32.3g protein;
5.1g fibre; 146mg sodium; low GI

tip Choose any pasta you like for this salad.

56.4g Carbs

tomato, bean and pasta soup

1 large brown onion (200g), chopped finely
1 cup (250ml) salt-reduced chicken stock
3 cups (750ml) water
410g (13 ounces) canned crushed tomatoes
1 teaspoon finely chopped fresh oregano
¾ cup (135g) wholemeal pasta spirals
410g (13 ounces) canned four-bean mix,
  rinsed, drained
2 medium zucchini (240g), chopped coarsely
2 tablespoons coarsely chopped fresh
  flat-leaf parsley

1 Cook onion and 2 tablespoons of the stock in large saucepan, stirring, until onion softens. Add remaining stock, the water, undrained tomatoes and oregano; bring to the boil. Add pasta; boil, uncovered, for 10 minutes.
2 Add beans and zucchini; simmer, uncovered, for about 5 minutes or until pasta is tender. Serve soup sprinkled with parsley. Serve with soy-linseed bread, if you like.

prep + cook time 50 minutes **serves** 4
nutritional count per serving 1.4g total fat
(0.2g saturated fat); 1045kJ (250 cal);
41.8g carbohydrate; 12.1g protein;
10.6g fibre; 424mg sodium; low GI

41.8g carbs

49

polenta with quick spinach sauté

1 cup (250ml) salt-reduced chicken stock
3 cups (750ml) water
1½ cups (255g) polenta
½ cup (40g) finely grated parmesan cheese
¼ cup finely chopped fresh flat-leaf parsley
2 teaspoons olive oil
1 clove garlic, crushed
500g (1 pound) spinach, trimmed, chopped coarsely

TOMATO MUSHROOM SAUCE
½ cup (125ml) water
1 medium brown onion (150g), chopped finely
1 clove garlic, crushed
410g (13 ounces) canned crushed tomatoes
1 tablespoon tomato paste
250g (8 ounces) button mushrooms, halved

1 Oil 20cm x 30cm (8-inch x 12-inch) rectangular pan.
2 Place stock and the water in medium saucepan; bring to the boil. Gradually stir polenta into the stock. Reduce heat; simmer, stirring, about 10 minutes or until polenta thickens. Stir in cheese and parsley; spread polenta into pan, cool 10 minutes. Cover, refrigerate 2 hours or until polenta is firm.
3 Meanwhile, make tomato mushroom sauce.
4 Turn polenta onto board; cut polenta into 16 triangles. Cook polenta on heated oiled grill plate (or grill or barbecue) until browned on both sides.
5 Heat oil in large frying pan, add garlic and spinach; cook, stirring, until spinach is wilted. Serve polenta and spinach with tomato mushroom sauce.

TOMATO MUSHROOM SAUCE Combine the water, onion and garlic in medium saucepan; cook, stirring, until onion softens and water evaporates. Add undrained tomatoes, paste and mushrooms; bring to the boil. Reduce heat; simmer, stirring, for about 5 minutes or until thickened.

prep + cook time 55 minutes (+ refrigeration)
serves 4
nutritional count per serving 7.7g total fat
(2.6g saturated fat); 1530kJ (366 cal);
52.5g carbohydrate; 16.6g protein;
9.1g fibre; 435mg sodium; low GI

curried lamb pasties

2 cups (300g) plain (all-purpose) flour
1 cup (160g) wholemeal plain (all-purpose) flour
⅓ cup (55g) polenta
1 tablespoon cumin seeds
125g (4 ounces) reduced-fat cream cheese, chopped coarsely
¾ cup (180ml) warm water, approximately
2 tablespoons low-fat milk, approximately

LAMB FILLING
250g (8 ounces) lean minced (ground) lamb
½ small kumara (orange sweet potato) (125g), grated coarsely
1 small brown onion (80g), chopped finely
½ small red capsicum (bell pepper) (75g), chopped finely
2 teaspoons green curry paste
¼ cup (60ml) beef stock
⅓ cup (40g) frozen peas
1 tablespoon finely chopped fresh mint

1 Sift flours into large bowl, stir in polenta and seeds; rub in cream cheese until mixture is crumbly. Stir in enough of the water to make ingredients cling together. Turn dough onto floured surface, knead gently until smooth. Wrap pastry in plastic wrap; refrigerate 30 minutes.
2 Meanwhile, make lamb filling.
3 Preheat oven to 200°C/400°F. Oil two oven trays.
4 Roll out half the pastry between sheets of baking paper until 2mm (⅛-inch) thick. Cut six 12cm (4¾-inch) rounds from pastry. Repeat with remaining pastry.
5 Place rounded tablespoons of cold lamb filling in centre of each pastry round; brush edges with a little milk. Fold in half, press edges together to seal. Place pasties about 5cm (2 inches) apart on trays; brush with a little extra milk. Bake about 25 minutes or until pastry is browned lightly.

LAMB FILLING Heat oiled medium frying pan; cook lamb, stirring, until browned. Add kumara, onion and capsicum; cook, stirring, until vegetables soften. Add curry paste; cook, stirring, until fragrant. Add stock and peas; cook, stirring, about 3 minutes or until liquid has evaporated. Remove from heat; stir in mint. Cool.

prep + cook time 1 hour 25 minutes (+ refrigeration)
makes 12
nutritional count per pasty 4.2g total fat
(1.9g saturated fat); 907kJ (217 cal);
32.2g carbohydrate; 10.6g protein;
3.2g fibre; 232mg sodium; low GI

carrot and lentil soup with caraway toasts

1 cup (250ml) salt-reduced vegetable stock
2 large brown onions (400g), chopped finely
2 cloves garlic, crushed
1 tablespoon ground cumin
6 large carrots (1kg), chopped coarsely
2 trimmed celery stalks (200g), chopped coarsely
1.375 litres (5½ cups) water
½ cup (100g) brown lentils
½ cup (125ml) buttermilk

CARAWAY TOASTS
6 slices (270g) wholemeal bread
⅓ cup (25g) finely grated parmesan cheese
2 cloves garlic, crushed
1 teaspoon caraway seeds
2 tablespoons finely chopped fresh
   flat-leaf parsley

1 Combine ½ cup (125ml) of the stock, onion, garlic and cumin in large saucepan; cook, stirring, until onion softens. Add carrot and celery; cook, stirring, for 5 minutes. Add remaining stock and the water; bring to the boil. Reduce heat; simmer, uncovered, about 20 minutes or until vegetables are tender. Cool mixture 10 minutes.
2 Blend or process mixture, in batches, until smooth. Return mixture to pan; add lentils. Simmer, uncovered, about 20 minutes or until lentils are tender.
3 Meanwhile, make caraway toasts.
4 Remove soup from heat; stir in buttermilk. Serve with caraway toasts.

CARAWAY TOASTS Preheat grill (broiler). Place bread, in single layer, on oven trays; cook under grill until browned lightly on one side. Sprinkle combined cheese, garlic, seeds and parsley over untoasted sides of bread; cook under grill until browned lightly. Cut in half.

prep + cook time 1 hour 10 minutes serves 6
nutritional count per serving 3.4g total fat
(1.4g saturated fat); 1091kJ (261 cal);
37.8g carbohydrate; 13.7g protein;
12.6g fibre; 433mg sodium; medium GI

asparagus frittata with rocket

cooking-oil spray
1 small red onion (100g), sliced thinly
170g (5½ ounces) asparagus, trimmed,
  chopped coarsely
2 eggs
2 egg whites
2 tablespoons low-fat cottage cheese
40g (1½ ounces) baby rocket (arugula) leaves
2 tablespoons lemon juice
2 teaspoons drained baby capers, rinsed

1 Preheat grill (broiler).
2 Spray small frying pan with cooking oil; cook
onion over heat, stirring, 1 minute. Add asparagus;
cook, stirring, 2 minutes.
3 Meanwhile, combine eggs, egg whites and
cheese in a medium jug. Pour over asparagus
mixture in pan. Cook, uncovered, about 5 minutes
or until frittata is browned underneath.
4 Place pan under grill (broiler) for about
5 minutes or until frittata is set.
5 Combine remaining ingredients in medium
bowl; serve frittata with salad.

prep + cook time 25 minutes serves 2
nutritional count per serving 6.3g total fat
(1.8g saturated fat); 614kJ (147 cal);
5.4g carbohydrate; 16.3g protein;
1.9g fibre; 188mg sodium; low GI

If the handle of your frying pan is not heatproof, cover it with
aluminium foil before placing it under the grill.
Frittata is delicious served warm, but if you like it cold, and
want to take it to work, make it the evening before, keep it in
the fridge, then wrap it in plastic the next morning.

ham, tomato and rocket pizza

2 large wholemeal pitta breads (160g)
2 tablespoons tomato paste
150g (4½ ounces) shaved salt-reduced lean ham
250g (8 ounces) cherry tomatoes, halved
¼ small red onion (25g), sliced thinly
⅓ cup (80g) low-fat ricotta cheese
30g (1 ounce) baby rocket (arugula) leaves
2 tablespoons finely shredded fresh basil

1 Preheat oven to 200°C/400°F.
2 Place bread on oven trays; spread with paste. Divide ham, tomato and onion between breads; top with dollops of cheese.
3 Bake about 10 minutes. Serve sprinkled with rocket and basil.

prep + cook time 25 minutes makes 2
nutritional count per pizza 8g total fat (3.5g saturated fat); 1559kJ (373 cal); 43.3g carbohydrate; 27.1g protein; 8.4g fibre; 841mg sodium; medium GI

chicken and bacon club sandwich

100g (3 ounces) chicken breast fillet
2 shortcut bacon slices (30g)
⅓ cup (65g) low-fat cottage cheese
4 slices (180g) rye bread, toasted
20g (¾ ounce) baby rocket (arugula) leaves
1 small tomato (90g), sliced thinly

1 Cook chicken in heated oiled small frying pan, until cooked through. Cover chicken; stand 5 minutes, then slice thinly.
2 Cook bacon in same pan until crisp.
3 Divide half the cheese between two toast slices; top with rocket, tomato, chicken, bacon, remaining cheese and toast.

prep + cook time 20 minutes serves 2
nutritional count per serving 5.6g total fat (1.2g saturated fat); 1459kJ (349 cal); 41.5g carbohydrate; 29.1g protein; 6.8g fibre; 762mg sodium; medium GI

tip This sandwich is at its best eaten warm, but if you don't have the right facilities to cook the chicken and bacon at lunch time, then cook the chicken and bacon in the morning and assemble the sandwich at work.

41.5g Carbs

spinach, tomato and prosciutto wholegrain pizza

⅓ cup (55g) finely cracked buckwheat
¼ cup (40g) burghul
¾ cup (180ml) warm water
1 teaspoon caster (superfine) sugar
8g (½ ounce) sachet dried yeast
1½ cups (225g) plain (all-purpose) flour
1 cup (160g) wholemeal plain (all-purpose) flour
½ cup (130g) bottled tomato pasta sauce
¾ cup (70g) coarsely grated mozzarella cheese
250g (8 ounces) red grape tomatoes, halved
6 slices prosciutto (90g), chopped coarsely
50g (1½ ounces) baby spinach leaves, trimmed

1 Combine buckwheat and burghul in medium heatproof bowl; cover with boiling water. Cover, stand 30 minutes. Rinse under cold water; drain buckwheat mixture thoroughly.
2 Combine the water, sugar and yeast in small jug. Stand in warm place about 10 minutes or until frothy.
3 Combine buckwheat mixture in large bowl with flours. Add yeast mixture; mix to a soft dough. Knead dough on floured surface about 10 minutes or until smooth and elastic. Place dough in lightly oiled large bowl; cover. Stand in warm place about 1 hour or until doubled in size.
4 Preheat oven to 220°C/425°F. Oil two pizza trays or oven trays.
5 Divide dough in half. Roll each portion on floured surface into 30cm (12-inch) round; place one on each tray.
6 Spread pizza bases with sauce; sprinkle with half the cheese then top with tomato and prosciutto. Sprinkle pizzas with remaining cheese. Bake about 20 minutes or until top is browned lightly and bases are crisp. Serve pizzas topped with spinach.

prep + cook time 45 minutes (+ standing) **serves** 6
nutritional count per serving 6g total fat (2.7g saturated fat); 1471kJ (352 cal); 57.4g carbohydrate; 16.9g protein; 7.1g fibre; 429mg sodium; medium GI

serving suggestion Serve with a green salad.

57.4g Carbs

mains

garlic prawns and buk choy with herbed rice

36 uncooked medium king prawns (shrimp) (1kg)
6 cloves garlic, crushed
2 teaspoons finely chopped fresh
   coriander (cilantro)
2 fresh small red thai (serrano) chillies,
   chopped finely
1 teaspoon light brown sugar
⅓ cup (80ml) lime juice
2 teaspoons peanut oil
1kg (2 pounds) baby buk choy,
   quartered lengthways
6 green onions (scallions), sliced thinly
1 tablespoon sweet chilli sauce

HERBED RICE
2 cups (400g) doongara rice
3 cups (750ml) water
2 tablespoons coarsely chopped fresh
   coriander (cilantro)
1 tablespoon coarsely chopped fresh mint
1 tablespoon coarsely chopped fresh
   flat-leaf parsley
1 teaspoon finely grated lime rind

1 Shell and devein prawns, leaving tails intact.
2 Combine prawns in large bowl with garlic,
coriander, chilli, sugar and juice.
3 Make herbed rice.
4 Meanwhile, heat oil in wok; stir-fry prawns, in
batches, until changed in colour. Remove from wok.
5 Add buk choy, onion, sauce and prawn marinade
to wok; stir-fry until buk choy is tender. Return
prawns to wok; stir-fry until hot. Serve prawn and
buk choy mixture with herbed rice.

HERBED RICE Rinse rice under cold water until
water runs clear; drain. Combine rice and the water
in large saucepan; bring to the boil. Reduce heat;
cook, covered, over low heat, 10 minutes. Remove
from heat; stand, covered, 10 minutes. Fluff rice
with fork. Stir in remaining ingredients.

prep + cook time 50 minutes serves 6
nutritional count per serving 2.9g total fat
(0.5g saturated fat); 1509kJ (361 cal);
56.6g carbohydrate; 23.9g protein;
3.8g fibre; 361mg sodium; medium GI

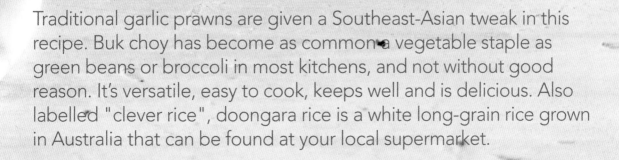

Traditional garlic prawns are given a Southeast-Asian tweak in this
recipe. Buk choy has become as common a vegetable staple as
green beans or broccoli in most kitchens, and not without good
reason. It's versatile, easy to cook, keeps well and is delicious. Also
labelled "clever rice", doongara rice is a white long-grain rice grown
in Australia that can be found at your local supermarket.

pork and cabbage rolls

8 large cabbage leaves, trimmed
1 teaspoon olive oil
1 large carrot (180g), grated coarsely
1 medium brown onion (150g), chopped finely
1 trimmed celery stalk (100g), chopped finely
2 cloves garlic, crushed
200g (6½ ounces) lean minced (ground) pork
1 tablespoon tomato paste
2 teaspoons ground cumin
1 teaspoon ground coriander
½ teaspoon ground allspice
2 cups (340g) cooked brown long-grain rice
50g (1½ ounces) baby rocket (arugula) leaves

TOMATO SAUCE
410 (13 ounces) canned crushed tomatoes
½ cup (125ml) salt-reduced chicken stock
2 cloves garlic, crushed
1 tablespoon finely chopped fresh flat-leaf parsley

1   Boil, steam or microwave cabbage leaves briefly until pliable; drain. Rinse under cold water; drain. Pat dry with absorbent paper.
2   Heat oil in large frying pan; cook carrot, onion, celery and garlic, stirring, about 5 minutes or until onion softens. Add pork and paste; cook, stirring, until pork is browned. Add spices; cook, stirring, until fragrant. Stir in rice; cool 10 minutes.
3   Divide rice mixture among leaves; roll firmly to enclose filling, folding in edges. Cook rolls, in single layer, in large baking-paper-lined bamboo steamer over large saucepan of simmering water, about 10 minutes or until heated through.
4   Meanwhile, make tomato sauce.
5   Serve cabbage rolls with tomato sauce and rocket.

TOMATO SAUCE   Combine undrained tomatoes, stock and garlic in small saucepan; bring to the boil. Reduce heat; simmer, uncovered, about 10 minutes or until thickened slightly. Stir in parsley.

prep + cook time 40 minutes serves 4
nutritional count per serving 3.8g total fat
(0.9g saturated fat); 1237kJ (296 cal);
43.4g carbohydrate; 17.4g protein;
8.3g fibre; 255mg sodium; low GI

You need to cook about ⅔ cup (130g) of brown rice for this recipe. Allspice, also known as pimento or jamaican pepper, is so-named because it tastes like a combination of clove, nutmeg, cinnamon and cumin – all spices. It is available from spice shops and supermarkets.

herb-stuffed chicken with tomato salad

600g (1¼ pounds) kipfler potatoes
cooking-oil spray
¼ cup finely chopped fresh basil
1 tablespoon finely chopped fresh oregano
2 teaspoons fresh lemon thyme
2 cloves garlic, crushed
1 tablespoon finely grated lemon rind
4 x 150g (4½ ounces) chicken breast fillets
4 slices prosciutto (60g)
250g (8 ounces) cherry tomatoes
250g (8 ounces) yellow cherry tomatoes
150g (4½ ounces) baby spinach leaves
½ cup coarsely chopped fresh basil
2 tablespoons red wine vinegar
2 teaspoons olive oil

1 Preheat oven to 220°C/425°F. Oil large baking dish.
2 Halve unpeeled potatoes lengthways. Place potato, in single layer, in dish; spray lightly with cooking-oil spray. Roast about 45 minutes or until browned lightly and tender.
3 Meanwhile, combine finely chopped basil, oregano, thyme, garlic and rind in small bowl. Halve chicken breasts horizontally, without cutting all the way through; open chicken breasts out flat onto board. Divide herb mixture among chicken pieces; fold to enclose filling, wrapping each with a prosciutto slice to secure.
4 Cook chicken in heated oiled large frying pan, about 10 minutes or until browned all over; place chicken on oven tray. Roast about 15 minutes, during the last 15 minutes of the potato cooking time, or until cooked through.
5 Meanwhile, cook tomatoes in same pan, over high heat, stirring, for 3 minutes. Combine tomatoes, spinach and coarsely chopped basil in large bowl with combined vinegar and oil. Serve salad with chicken and potatoes. Sprinkle chicken with extra lemon thyme leaves, if you like.

prep + cook time 1 hour 10 minutes serves 4
nutritional count per serving 6.3g total fat
(1.4g saturated fat); 1400kJ (335 cal);
23.2g carbohydrate; 41.5g protein;
6.6g fibre; 370mg sodium; medium GI

chilli coriander lamb and barley salad

1 tablespoon coriander seeds, crushed lightly
½ teaspoon dried chilli flakes
2 cloves garlic, crushed
600g (1¼ pounds) lamb backstraps
1 cup (200g) pearl barley
¼ teaspoon ground turmeric
⅓ cup each loosely packed fresh mint
  and coriander (cilantro) leaves
1 small red onion (100g), chopped finely
250g (8 ounces) cherry tomatoes, halved
¼ cup (60ml) lemon juice
2 teaspoons olive oil

1 Combine seeds, chilli and garlic in medium bowl, add lamb; toss to coat lamb in mixture. Cover, refrigerate 30 minutes.
2 Meanwhile, cook barley in large saucepan of boiling water, about 20 minutes or until tender; drain. Rinse under cold water; drain.
3 Cook lamb on heated oiled grill plate (or grill or barbecue) until cooked as desired. Cover lamb; stand 5 minutes, then slice thickly.
4 Meanwhile, combine remaining ingredients in large bowl, add barley; stir to combine. Serve barley salad with lamb.

prep + cook time 50 minutes (+ refrigeration)
serves 4
nutritional count per serving 9.7g total fat (2.6g saturated fat); 1597k.I (382 cal); 34.1g carbohydrate; 35g protein; 7.6g fibre; 122mg sodium; low GI

linguine marinara

150g (4½ ounces) linguine pasta
400g (12½ ounces) marinara mix
1 small brown onion (80g), chopped finely
2 cloves garlic, crushed
1 fresh small red thai (serrano) chilli, chopped finely
410g (13 ounces) canned diced tomatoes
¼ cup (60ml) water
⅓ cup coarsely chopped fresh flat-leaf parsley

1 Cook pasta in large saucepan of boiling water until tender; drain.
2 Meanwhile, cook marinara mix in heated large frying pan, stirring, for 2 minutes; remove from pan.
3 Add onion, garlic and chilli to same heated, lightly oiled pan; cook, stirring, about 5 minutes or until onion softens. Add undrained tomatoes and the water; cook, stirring, 5 minutes. Return seafood to pan; cook, stirring occasionally, about 2 minutes or until heated through. Stir in parsley.
4 Serve pasta topped with marinara sauce.

prep + cook time 20 minutes serves 2
nutritional count per serving 7.2g total fat (1.8g saturated fat); 2387kJ (571 cal); 61.9g carbohydrate; 60.1g protein; 6.4g fibre; 551mg sodium; low GI

tips This is a really simple recipe. There's only one thing to be careful of – don't overcook the seafood – if you do, it will be tough and leathery. Use any pasta shape you like – and don't overcook it either. Cooked pasta with a little bit of bite left in it is better for your digestive system.

Wear disposable gloves when handling cooked beetroot. When you squeeze the warm beetroot, the skin will burst and peel away easily.

wholemeal beetroot and goat's cheese pizzas

¼ cup (45g) cracked buckwheat
½ cup (125ml) warm water
½ teaspoon caster (superfine) sugar
1 teaspoon dried yeast
¾ cup (110g) plain (all-purpose) flour
¾ cup (120g) wholemeal plain (all-purpose) flour
2 large beetroot (beets) (400g)
8 shallots (200g), peeled
½ cup (140g) tomato paste
120g (4 ounces) goat's cheese, crumbled
40g (1½ ounces) baby rocket (arugula) leaves

1 Place buckwheat in small heatproof bowl; cover with boiling water. Stand 30 minutes, covered. Rinse under cold water; drain.
2 Combine the water, sugar and yeast in small jug, cover; stand in a warm place about 10 minutes or until frothy.
3 Combine buckwheat and sifted flours in large bowl. Add yeast mixture; mix to a soft dough. Knead dough on floured surface about 10 minutes or until smooth and elastic. Place dough in oiled large bowl. Cover; stand in warm place about 45 minutes or until doubled in size.
4 Meanwhile, preheat oven to 220°C/425°F. Oil two large oven trays.
5 Trim leaves from beetroot, wrap unpeeled beetroot in foil; place in small shallow baking dish. Roast beetroot 20 minutes. Add shallots to dish; roast about 30 minutes or until vegetables are tender. Cool 10 minutes. Peel beetroot; chop coarsely. Cut shallots into small wedges.
6 Divide dough into four. Roll each piece into 15cm (6-inch) rounds; place on trays.
7 Bake bases 10 minutes. Remove from oven; spread bases with paste, sprinkle with cheese. Bake bases about 8 minutes or until crisp.
8 Top pizzas with beetroot, shallots and rocket.

prep + cook time 50 minutes (+ standing) makes 4
nutritional count per pizza 6.4g total fat
(3.3g saturated fat); 1613kJ (386 cal);
61.3g carbohydrate; 15.6g protein;
9.5g fibre; 440mg sodium; medium GI

  61.3g carbs

moroccan kebabs with preserved lemon couscous

½ cup finely chopped fresh coriander (cilantro)
2 cloves garlic, crushed
1 tablespoon olive oil
2 fresh small red thai (serrano) chillies,
  chopped finely
¼ cup (60ml) lemon juice
600g (1¼ pounds) skinless firm white fish fillets,
  cut into 3cm (1¼-inch) pieces
1 cup (250ml) salt-reduced chicken stock
½ cup (125ml) water
1½ cups (300g) couscous
½ cup firmly packed fresh coriander
  (cilantro) leaves
1 tablespoon finely chopped preserved lemon
¼ cup (35g) toasted slivered almonds

1 Combine chopped coriander, garlic, oil, chilli and juice in small bowl. Place half the coriander mixture in large bowl, add fish; toss to coat fish in mixture. Thread fish onto eight skewers; place kebabs on tray. Cover, refrigerate 45 minutes.
2 Cook kebabs on heated oiled grill plate (or grill or barbecue) about 5 minutes or until cooked as desired.
3 Meanwhile, bring stock and the water to the boil in medium saucepan; remove from heat. Add couscous to stock, cover; stand about 5 minutes or until liquid is absorbed, fluffing with fork occasionally. Add remaining coriander mixture, coriander leaves, lemon and nuts; stir to combine. Serve couscous with kebabs.

prep + cook time 35 minutes (+ refrigeration)
serves 4
nutritional count per serving 12.4g total fat (2g saturated fat); 2220kJ (531 cal); 59.5g carbohydrate; 42.8g protein; 2g fibre; 294mg sodium; low GI

serving suggestion Serve with a rocket (arugula) or spinach salad.

You will need to soak eight 25cm (10-inch) bamboo skewers in water for at least an hour before using to prevent them from splintering or scorching during the cooking process.

You could stir some finely chopped and seeded cucumber into the remaining yogurt.

grilled paprika chicken with raisin pilaf

1.2kg (2½ pounds) chicken breast fillets
2 tablespoons lemon juice
3 cloves garlic, crushed
1 teaspoon sweet paprika
1 teaspoon ground cinnamon
½ teaspoon hot paprika
2 teaspoons olive oil
1 medium brown onion (150g), chopped finely
3½ cups (700g) basmati rice
1 litre (4 cups) salt-reduced chicken stock
3 cups (750ml) water
1 cup (280g) low-fat greek-style yogurt
½ cup (80g) coarsely chopped raisins
1½ cups coarsely chopped fresh
  coriander (cilantro)

1 Combine chicken, juice, garlic and spices in large bowl. Cover, refrigerate 2 hours.
2 Heat oil in large saucepan; cook onion, stirring, until softened. Add rice; stir to coat in onion mixture. Add stock and the water; bring to the boil. Reduce heat; simmer, covered, stirring occasionally, about 25 minutes or until rice is tender. Remove from heat; stand, covered, 5 minutes.
3 Meanwhile, cook chicken on heated oiled grill plate (or grill or barbecue), brushing with ¼ cup (70g) of the yogurt, until browned all over and cooked through. Cover chicken; stand 5 minutes, then slice thickly.
4 Stir raisins and coriander into pilaf. Serve pilaf with chicken and remaining yogurt.

prep + cook time 45 minutes (+ refrigeration)
serves 8
nutritional count per serving 4.2g total fat
(1.2g saturated fat); 2090kJ (500 cal);
71.2g carbohydrate; 42.2g protein;
1.6g fibre; 333mg sodium; medium GI

serving suggestion Serve chicken with crusty wholemeal bread rolls.

lime and chilli fish baked in banana leaves

2 large banana leaves
4 x 10cm (4-inch) sticks fresh lemon grass
3 fresh small red thai (serrano) chillies, sliced thinly
4 cloves garlic, crushed
1 tablespoon finely grated lime rind
⅓ cup (80ml) lime juice
2 tablespoons finely grated fresh ginger
1 cup coarsely chopped fresh coriander (cilantro)
⅔ cup (160ml) light coconut milk
8 x 150g (4½ ounces) firm white fish fillets
2½ cups (500g) doongara rice
1.25 litres (5 cups) water
4 green onions (scallions), sliced thinly

1 Preheat oven 220°C/425°F.
2 Trim each banana leaf into four 30cm (12-inch) squares. Using metal tongs, dip one square at a time into large saucepan of boiling water; remove immediately. Rinse under cold running water; pat dry with absorbent paper. Banana leaf squares should be soft and pliable.
3 Halve lemon grass sticks lengthways. Combine chilli, garlic, rind, juice, ginger, coriander and coconut milk in small bowl.
4 Centre each fish fillet on banana leaf square. Top with lemon grass; drizzle with chilli mixture. Fold square over fish to enclose; secure each parcel with kitchen string.
5 Rinse rice under cold water until water runs clear; drain. Combine rice and the water in large saucepan; bring to the boil. Reduce heat; cook, covered, over low heat, 10 minutes. Remove from heat; stand, covered, 10 minutes. Fluff rice with fork. Stir in onion.
6 Meanwhile, place parcels, in single layer, in large baking dish. Roast about 10 minutes or until fish is cooked as desired. Serve fish parcels with rice.

prep + cook time 50 minutes serves 8
nutritional count per serving 2.7g total fat
(1.5g saturated fat); 1542kJ (369 cal);
50.4g carbohydrate; 34.1g protein;
1.1g fibre; 221mg sodium; medium GI

Let your guests unwrap their own fish "package" at the table so that the spicy aroma wafts up from the plates and enlivens their appetites. Foil can be used if banana leaves are unavailable. Many supermarkets and greengrocers sell bundles of trimmed banana-leaf squares; they can also be used as placemats for an Asian meal.

The food of Thailand takes first prize in the popularity stakes these days and no wonder: quick and easy to prepare, delicious recipes such as this are every cook's dream… and their fresh vegetable content makes them healthy too. You'll need to grate the rind from the lime before you juice it.

Thai basil has slightly smaller leaves than common basil and a strong, somewhat aniseed, flavour.

thai basil chicken stir-fry

1 teaspoon sesame oil
¼ cup (60ml) salt-reduced soy sauce
¼ cup (60ml) lime juice
2 tablespoons honey
2 fresh small red thai (serrano) chillies, sliced thinly
2 teaspoons cornflour (cornstarch)
850g (1¾ pounds) chicken breast fillets, sliced thinly
1½ cups (300g) doongara rice
3 cups (750ml) water
1 tablespoon peanut oil
3 cloves garlic, crushed
2 large red onions (400g), sliced thinly
240g (7½ ounces) fresh baby corn
¼ cup (60ml) water, extra
2 teaspoons finely grated lime rind
3 cups (240g) bean sprouts
2 cups loosely packed fresh thai basil leaves
1 cup loosely packed fresh coriander (cilantro) leaves

1 Combine sesame oil, sauce, juice, honey, chilli and cornflour in large bowl. Add chicken; toss to coat chicken in marinade. Cover, refrigerate 1 hour.
2 Rinse rice under cold water until water runs clear; drain. Bring the water to the boil, covered, in large saucepan; add rice. Cook, covered, over low heat, 10 minutes. Remove from heat; stand, covered, 10 minutes. Fluff rice with fork.
3 Meanwhile, drain chicken over medium bowl; reserve marinade.
4 Heat half the peanut oil in wok; stir-fry chicken, in batches, until browned all over. Remove from wok. Heat remaining peanut oil in wok; stir-fry garlic, onion and corn until tender. Return chicken to wok with reserved marinade, the extra water and rind; stir-fry until sauce boils and chicken is cooked.
5 Remove from heat; add sprouts and herbs. Serve stir-fry with rice.

prep + cook time 40 minutes (+ refrigeration)
serves 6
nutritional count per serving 7g total fat (1.5g saturated fat); 1977kJ (473 cal); 59.7g carbohydrate; 39.7g protein; 4.5g fibre; 424mg sodium; medium GI

serving suggestion Serve with lime wedges.

prawn and basil risotto

500g (1 pound) uncooked medium king
  prawns (shrimp)
1 cup (250ml) salt-reduced chicken stock
1 cup (250ml) dry white wine
3 cups (750ml) water
1 trimmed celery stalk (100g), chopped finely
1 small brown onion (80g), chopped finely
1 cup (200g) arborio rice
1 cup (170g) cooked brown long-grain rice
2 medium tomatoes (300g), seeded,
  chopped finely
½ cup loosely packed fresh basil leaves
2 tablespoons finely chopped fresh
  flat-leaf parsley

1 Shell and devein prawns, leaving tails intact.
2 Bring stock, wine and 2 cups (500ml) of the water
to the boil in medium saucepan. Reduce heat;
simmer, covered.
3 Meanwhile, cook celery, onion and the
remaining water in large saucepan, stirring, about
10 minutes or until water has evaporated.
Stir in arborio rice.

4 Add ½ cup (125ml) of the simmering stock
mixture; cook, stirring, over low heat until liquid is
absorbed. Continue adding stock mixture, in ½-cup
(125ml) batches, stirring until liquid is absorbed
after each addition. Total cooking time should be
about 35 minutes or until rice is tender.
5 After last addition of stock mixture, add prawns
and brown rice; cook, stirring, until prawns are
changed in colour. Remove from heat; stir in
tomato and herbs.

prep + cook time 50 minutes serves 4
nutritional count per serving 1.3g total fat
(0.3g saturated fat); 1572kJ (376 cal);
59g carbohydrate; 19.3g protein;
2.5g fibre; 418mg sodium; medium GI

tip You will need to cook about ½ cup (100g)
brown long-grain rice for this recipe.

warm pasta and lamb salad

500g (1 pound) lamb fillets
⅓ cup (80ml) lemon juice
2 tablespoons finely chopped fresh rosemary
1 tablespoon dry red wine
1 tablespoon sweet chilli sauce
1 tablespoon olive oil
1 teaspoon light brown sugar
1 clove garlic, crushed
4 medium egg (plum) tomatoes (300g), quartered
350g (11 ounces) wholemeal spiral pasta
½ cup (125ml) salt-reduced beef stock
2 tablespoons coarsely chopped fresh
  flat-leaf parsley
500g (1 pound) spinach, trimmed,
  chopped coarsely

1 Combine lamb, juice, rosemary, wine, sauce, half
the oil, sugar and garlic in medium bowl. Cover,
refrigerate 2 hours.
2 Preheat oven to 180°C/350°F. Oil oven tray.

3 Place tomato in single layer on tray. Bake about
20 minutes.
4 Cook pasta in large saucepan of boiling water,
until tender; drain.
5 Meanwhile, drain lamb over medium bowl;
reserve marinade. Heat remaining oil in medium
frying pan; cook lamb, until browned all over and
cooked as desired. Cover lamb; stand 5 minutes,
then slice thinly.
6 Add reserved marinade, stock and parsley to
same pan; bring to the boil.
7 Combine tomato, pasta, lamb, marinade mixture
and spinach in large bowl.

prep + cook time 50 minutes (+ refrigeration)
serves 4
nutritional count per serving 12.2g total fat
(2.7g saturated fat); 2249kJ (538 cal);
57.9g carbohydrate; 40.2g protein;
13.3g fibre; 310mg sodium; low GI

lentil patties with spicy eggplant sauce

2 medium potatoes (400g), chopped coarsely
⅔ cup (130g) red lentils
1 medium red capsicum (bell pepper) (200g)
2 teaspoons olive oil
1 medium brown onion (150g), chopped finely
2 cloves garlic, crushed
2 tablespoons water
1 trimmed celery stalk (100g), chopped finely
2 trimmed medium silver beet (swiss chard) leaves
  (160g), shredded
¼ cup (40g) roasted pine nuts, chopped coarsely
1½ cups (105g) stale wholemeal breadcrumbs
2 teaspoons coarsely chopped fresh
  coriander (cilantro)
1 tablespoon coarsely chopped fresh
  flat-leaf parsley
½ cup (50g) packaged breadcrumbs,
  approximately
2 teaspoons vegetable oil

SPICY EGGPLANT SAUCE
1 large eggplant (500g)
1 clove garlic, crushed
2 tablespoons lemon juice
1 tablespoon sweet chilli sauce
¼ cup (70g) low-fat natural yogurt
1 tablespoon coarsely chopped fresh
  flat-leaf parsley

1 Make spicy eggplant sauce.
2 Meanwhile, boil, steam or microwave potato until tender; drain. Mash potato until smooth. Cook lentils in medium saucepan of boiling water, about 8 minutes or until tender; drain.
3 Quarter capsicum; discard seeds and membranes. Roast capsicum under hot grill, skin-side-up, until skin blisters and blackens. Cover capsicum pieces with plastic or paper 5 minutes; peel away skin then chop coarsely.
4 Heat olive oil in medium frying pan; cook onion and garlic, stirring, until softened. Add the water and celery; cook, stirring, until water has almost evaporated. Add silver beet; cook, stirring, until wilted.
5 Combine mashed potato, lentils, capsicum, onion mixture, pine nuts, stale breadcrumbs and herbs in bowl. Shape mixture into six patties; toss in packaged breadcrumbs, place on tray. Cover, refrigerate 1 hour.
6 Heat vegetable oil in large frying pan; cook patties about 2 minutes each side or until browned and heated through. Serve patties with spicy eggplant sauce.

SPICY EGGPLANT SAUCE Preheat oven to 180°C/350°F. Halve eggplant lengthways, place cut-side down on oiled oven tray. Roast about 45 minutes or until eggplant softens; cool. Scoop out flesh, discard skin. Blend or process eggplant with garlic, juice, sauce and yogurt until combined. Stir in parsley.

prep + cook time 1 hour 30 minutes (+ refrigeration)
serves 6
nutritional count per serving 9.6g total fat
(0.9g saturated fat); 1237kJ (296 cal);
34.6g carbohydrate; 13.4g protein;
2.7g fibre; 277mg sodium; medium GI

serving suggestion Serve with a green salad.

steaks with capsicum salsa

600g (1¼ pounds) kipfler potatoes
cooking-oil spray
1 small red capsicum (bell pepper) (150g),
   chopped finely
1 small green capsicum (bell pepper) (150g),
   chopped finely
1 medium red onion (170g), chopped finely
1 large tomato (220g), seeded, chopped finely
1 tablespoon coarsely chopped fresh
   coriander (cilantro)
¼ cup (60ml) oil-free french dressing
2 cloves garlic, crushed
1 teaspoon ground cumin
4 x 150g (4½-ounce) beef eye fillet steaks
60g (2 ounces) baby rocket (arugula) leaves

1 Preheat oven to 220°C/425°F. Oil large baking dish.
2 Halve unpeeled potatoes lengthways. Place potato, in single layer, in dish; spray lightly with cooking-oil spray. Roast about 45 minutes or until browned lightly and tender.
3 Meanwhile, combine capsicum, onion, tomato, coriander, french dressing, garlic and cumin in medium bowl.
4 Cook beef on heated oiled grill plate (or grill or barbecue) until browned both sides and cooked as desired. Cover beef; stand 5 minutes. Serve beef with capsicum salsa, roasted potatoes and rocket.

prep + cook time 1 hour serves 4
nutritional count per serving 10.2g total fat
(3.6g saturated fat); 1559kJ (373 cal);
28g carbohydrate; 38.9g protein;
5g fibre; 261mg sodium; medium GI

tofu and spinach stir-fry

350g (11 ounces) firm tofu
2 tablespoons hoisin sauce
1 tablespoon oyster sauce
1 tablespoon salt-reduced soy sauce
1 teaspoon finely grated fresh ginger
2 cloves garlic, crushed
2 teaspoons peanut oil
1 large brown onion (200g), sliced thinly
1 medium red capsicum (bell pepper) (200g),
   sliced thinly
200g (6½ ounces) snow peas
350g (11 ounces) spinach, trimmed,
   chopped coarsely
¼ cup (60ml) water
350g (11 ounces) fresh egg noodles

1 Cut tofu into 2cm (¾-inch) cubes; spread, in single layer, on tray lined with absorbent paper. Cover tofu with more absorbent paper; stand 10 minutes.
2 Combine sauces, ginger, garlic and tofu in medium bowl. Cover, refrigerate for 2 hours.
3 Heat oil in wok; stir-fry onion and capsicum until onion softens. Add peas, spinach, the water and tofu mixture; stir-fry until spinach wilts.
4 Meanwhile, place noodles in large heatproof bowl, cover with boiling water; stand until tender, drain.
5 Divide noodles among serving bowls, top with tofu and vegetable mixture.

prep + cook time 25 minutes
(+ standing & refrigeration)
serves 4
nutritional count per serving 6.2g total fat
(1g saturated fat); 1676kJ (401 cal);
60.4g carbohydrate; 20.6g protein;
9g fibre; 626mg sodium; low GI

eggplant, tomato and leek lasagne

3 medium eggplants (900g)
1 large brown onion (200g), chopped finely
4 cloves garlic, crushed
3 large tomatoes (660g), chopped coarsely
2 tablespoons tomato paste
¼ cup finely shredded fresh basil
½ cup (125ml) water
2 teaspoons olive oil
2 medium leeks (700g), sliced thinly
1 tablespoon light brown sugar
4 fresh lasagne sheets (200g)
1 cup (125g) coarsely grated reduced-fat
  cheddar cheese

1 Slice eggplants lengthways into 1cm (½-inch) slices. Cook, in batches, on heated oiled grill plate (or grill or barbecue) until browned lightly and tender.
2 Heat oiled medium frying pan; cook onion and half the garlic, stirring, until softened. Stir in tomato, paste and basil; bring to the boil, stirring. Reduce heat, simmer, uncovered, about 10 minutes or until sauce thickens. Blend or process tomato mixture with the water until almost smooth.
3 Heat oil in same pan; cook leek and remaining garlic, stirring, until softened. Add sugar; cook, stirring, about 5 minutes or until browned lightly.
4 Preheat oven to 200°C/400°F. Oil deep 20cm x 30cm (8-inch x 12-inch) (10-cup) ovenproof dish.
5 Cut one lasagne sheet to cover base of dish; top with a quarter of the eggplant, a quarter of the leek mixture, a quarter of the tomato mixture and a quarter of the cheese. Repeat to make three layers. Bake about 50 minutes. Stand 10 minutes.

prep + cook time 1 hour serves 6
nutritional count per serving 6.5g total fat
(2.4g saturated fat); 1091kJ (261 cal);
31.4g carbohydrate; 14.7g protein;
9.1g fibre; 300mg sodium; low GI

serving suggestion Serve with a garden salad.

chicken and pumpkin curry

½ cup (100g) brown long-grain rice
1 small red onion (100g), chopped finely
2 tablespoons finely chopped coriander (cilantro)
  root and stem mixture
¼ cup firmly packed fresh coriander
  (cilantro) leaves
2 fresh long red chillies, chopped coarsely
2 cloves garlic, crushed
5cm (2-inch) piece fresh ginger (25g), grated finely
1 teaspoon ground turmeric
1 cup (250ml) salt-reduced chicken stock
180g (5½ ounces) chicken breast fillet, sliced thinly
¼ cup (60ml) light coconut milk
150g (4½ ounces) butternut pumpkin, cut into
  1cm (½-inch) pieces
115g (3½ ounces) baby corn, chopped coarsely
1 cup (80g) bean sprouts
2 tablespoons fresh coriander (cilantro) leaves, extra

1 Cook rice in large saucepan of boiling water
until tender; drain.
2 Meanwhile, blend onion, coriander root and
stem mixture, coriander leaves, chilli, garlic, ginger
and turmeric until smooth.
3 Cook paste in medium saucepan, stirring, until
fragrant. Add stock, chicken and coconut milk;
bring to the boil. Reduce heat; simmer, covered,
10 minutes.
4 Add pumpkin and corn to pan; simmer,
uncovered, about 10 minutes or until pumpkin
is tender.
5 Serve rice topped with curry, sprouts and
extra coriander.

prep + cook time 45 minutes **serves** 2
nutritional count per serving 8.7g total fat
(4.6g saturated fat); 1973kJ (472 cal);
58.4g carbohydrate; 32.7g protein;
8.3g fibre; 368mg sodium; medium GI

tip Brown rice takes about 30 minutes to cook,
sometimes less depending on how crunchy you like
it. If you want takeaway curry, the whole recipe can
be made a day ahead, then reheated in a
microwave oven at lunch time.

Traditional to North Africa, a tagine is an aromatic casserole, usually cooked and served in an earthenware dish, also called a tagine.

pumpkin and split pea tagine

1 cup (200g) green split peas
1 tablespoon olive oil
1 medium brown onion (150g), chopped finely
2 cloves garlic, crushed
2 teaspoons ground coriander
2 teaspoons ground cumin
2 teaspoons ground ginger
1 teaspoon sweet paprika
1 teaspoon ground allspice
1kg (2 pounds) pumpkin, cut into 3cm
  (1¼-inch) pieces
410g (13 ounces) canned crushed tomatoes
1 cup (250ml) water
1 cup (250ml) salt-reduced vegetable stock
2 tablespoons honey
200g (6½ ounces) green beans, trimmed,
  chopped coarsely
¼ cup coarsely chopped fresh coriander (cilantro)

1 Cook split peas in medium saucepan of boiling water, until tender; drain. Rinse peas under cold water; drain.
2 Meanwhile, heat oil in large saucepan; cook onion, stirring, until softened. Add garlic and spices; cook, stirring, about 2 minutes or until fragrant. Add pumpkin; stir to coat pumpkin in spice mixture.
3 Stir in undrained tomatoes, the water and stock; bring to the boil. Reduce heat; simmer, uncovered, about 20 minutes or until pumpkin is tender. Stir in honey, beans and split peas; simmer, uncovered, about 5 minutes or until beans are tender. Remove from heat; stir in coriander.

prep + cook time 55 minutes **serves** 4
nutritional count per serving 7g total fat
(1.5g saturated fat); 1484kJ (355 cal);
55.9g carbohydrate; 19.1g protein;
11g fibre; 323mg sodium; medium GI

serving suggestion Serve with steamed couscous.

brown rice pilaf

1 small kumara (orange sweet potato) (200g),
  chopped coarsely
cooking-oil spray
½ cup (125ml) salt-reduced vegetable stock
1 cup (250ml) water
2 teaspoons olive oil
1 medium brown onion (150g), chopped finely
2 cloves garlic, crushed
2 trimmed celery stalks (200g), sliced thinly
150g (4½ ounces) button mushrooms, halved
¾ cup (150g) brown medium-grain rice
1 tablespoon finely grated lemon rind
½ cup loosely packed fresh flat-leaf parsley leaves

1 Preheat oven to 180°C/350°F.
2 Place kumara on baking-paper-lined oven tray; spray lightly with cooking-oil spray. Roast about 25 minutes or until tender.
3 Meanwhile, place stock and the water in small saucepan; bring to the boil. Reduce heat; simmer, covered.
4 Heat oil in medium saucepan; cook onion, garlic and celery, stirring, until onion softens. Add mushrooms and rice; cook, stirring, 2 minutes. Add stock, reduce heat; simmer, covered, about 50 minutes or until stock is absorbed and rice is tender. Stir in kumara, rind and parsley.

prep + cook time 1 hour 15 minutes **serves** 2
nutritional count per serving 7.6g total fat (1.1g saturated fat); 1944kJ (465 cal); 80.9g carbohydrate; 12.5g protein; 10g fibre; 352mg sodium; medium GI

chicken, lentil and spinach pasta

2 teaspoons olive oil
1 small brown onion (80g), chopped finely
2 cloves garlic, crushed
150g (4½ ounces) lean minced (ground) chicken
½ cup (100g) red lentils
2 cups (500ml) salt-reduced chicken stock
¾ cup (180ml) water
2 tablespoons tomato paste
250g (8 ounces) baby spinach leaves
300g (9½ ounces) shell pasta

1 Heat oil in medium saucepan; cook onion and garlic, stirring, until onion softens. Add chicken; cook, stirring, until browned. Stir in lentils, stock, the water and paste; bring to the boil. Reduce heat; simmer, uncovered, about 10 minutes or until lentils are tender. Add spinach; stir until wilted.
2 Meanwhile, cook pasta in large saucepan of boiling water, until tender; drain.
3 Combine pasta and chicken sauce in large bowl.

prep + cook time 35 minutes **serves** 4
nutritional count per serving 4.6g total fat
(0.9g saturated fat); 1777kJ (425 cal);
65.1g carbohydrate; 26.4g protein;
8.6g fibre; 418mg sodium; low GI

pasta primavera with poached salmon

300g (9½ ounces) fettuccine pasta
1.25 litres (5 cups) water
440g (14 ounces) salmon fillets
2 sprigs fresh dill
6 black peppercorns
2 teaspoons finely grated lemon rind
2 teaspoons olive oil
2 cloves garlic, crushed
1 medium red onion (170g), sliced thinly
170g (5½ ounces) asparagus, halved crossways
½ cup (60g) frozen peas
150g (4½ ounces) snow peas, trimmed, halved
2 tablespoons lemon juice
2 teaspoons finely chopped fresh dill
2 tablespoons coarsely chopped fresh
  flat-leaf parsley

1 Cook pasta in large saucepan of boiling water, until tender; drain.
2 Meanwhile, combine the water, fish, dill sprigs, peppercorns and half the rind in large saucepan; bring to the boil. Reduce heat; simmer, uncovered, 8 minutes, turning fish halfway through cooking time. Remove fish from poaching liquid; discard liquid. When cool enough to handle, remove and discard skin; flake fish into medium bowl.
3 Heat oil in same cleaned pan; cook garlic, onion and asparagus, stirring, until asparagus is tender. Add peas, snow peas, juice, pasta, remaining rind, and fish; stir until hot. Remove from heat; stir in herbs.

prep + cook time 40 minutes serves 4
nutritional count per serving 11.2g total fat
(2.2g saturated fat); 2015kJ (482 cal);
57.7g carbohydrate; 33.7g protein;
5.8g fibre; 60mg sodium; low GI

Did you know? Salmon is richer than tuna in essential omega-3 fatty acids. When going for omega-3s you can also boost intakes with fortified foods, just look on the label for the terms DHA or EPA, which describe the best form of omegas.

lemon chilli pork with italian brown rice salad

2 teaspoons finely grated lemon rind
2 tablespoons lemon juice
½ teaspoon dried chilli flakes
2 teaspoons olive oil
4 x 240g (7½-ounce) pork cutlets

ITALIAN BROWN RICE SALAD
1 cup (200g) brown long-grain rice
1 medium red capsicum (bell pepper) (200g),
  chopped finely
½ cup (60g) seeded black olives,
  chopped coarsely
2 tablespoons drained capers, rinsed, drained
½ cup coarsely chopped fresh basil
⅓ cup coarsely chopped fresh flat-leaf parsley
2 tablespoons lemon juice
2 teaspoons olive oil

1 Combine rind, juice, chilli, oil and pork in
medium bowl. Cover, refrigerate for 2 hours.
2 Meanwhile, make italian brown rice salad.
3 Cook pork on heated oiled grill plate (or grill or
barbecue), over medium heat, until browned both
sides and cooked as desired. Cover pork; stand
5 minutes. Serve pork with rice salad.

ITALIAN BROWN RICE SALAD Cook rice in large
saucepan of boiling water, until tender; drain. Rinse
under cold water; drain. Combine rice and
remaining ingredients in large bowl.

prep + cook time 1 hour 10 minutes (+ refrigeration)
serves 4
nutritional count per serving 8.7g total fat
(1.8g saturated fat); 1768kJ (423 cal);
45g carbohydrate; 38.6g protein;
2.8g fibre; 256mg sodium; medium GI

serving suggestion Serve with a rocket (arugula) or
spinach salad.

Various combinations of rice and lentils are eaten throughout the Middle East and India, with perhaps the two most well-known versions being Lebanese mujadara and Indian kitcheree. Our Egyptian take on this homely dish, however, adds delicious "oomph" to the rice-lentil theme with its fragrantly spicy caramelised onion and piquant chilli sauce.

koshari

1½ cups (300g) brown lentils
¾ cup (150g) doongara rice
1 cup coarsely chopped fresh flat-leaf parsley

CARAMELISED ONION
1 tablespoon olive oil
5 large brown onions (1kg), sliced thinly
1½ teaspoons ground allspice
1 teaspoon ground coriander
2 teaspoons white sugar

TOMATO CHILLI SAUCE
2 teaspoons olive oil
3 cloves garlic, crushed
½ teaspoon ground cumin
½ teaspoon dried chilli flakes
⅓ cup (80ml) white vinegar
1⅔ cups (410ml) canned tomato juice

1 Make the caramelised onion. Make the tomato chilli sauce.
2 Meanwhile, cook lentils and rice, separately, in medium saucepans of boiling water, until both are tender; drain.
3 Remove half the caramelised onion from pan; reserve. Add lentils and rice to remaining onion in pan; stir until hot. Remove from heat; stir in half the parsley.
4 Divide koshari among serving bowls; top with reserved caramelised onion, remaining parsley and tomato chilli sauce.

CARAMELISED ONION Heat oil in large frying pan; cook onion, allspice and coriander, stirring, until onion softens. Add sugar; cook, stirring occasionally, about 30 minutes or until onion caramelises.

TOMATO CHILLI SAUCE Heat oil in small saucepan; cook garlic, cumin and chilli, stirring, until fragrant. Add vinegar and juice; bring to the boil. Boil, uncovered, 2 minutes.

prep + cook time 1 hour serves 4
nutritional count per serving 8.8g total fat (1.2g saturated fat); 2157kJ (516 cal); 77.5g carbohydrate; 25g protein; 15.2g fibre; 349mg sodium; low GI

serving suggestion Serve koshari with steamed green vegetables.

seared tuna with chilled soba

200g (6½ ounces) dried soba noodles
¼ cup (60ml) mirin
2 tablespoons kecap manis
1 tablespoon cooking sake
2 teaspoons white sugar
5cm (2-inch) piece fresh ginger (25g), grated finely
1 clove garlic, crushed
4 tuna steaks (600g)
1 sheet toasted seaweed (yaki-nori), sliced thinly
2 green onions (scallions), chopped finely
1 teaspoon sesame oil
2 tablespoons pickled ginger, sliced thinly

1 Cook noodles in large saucepan of boiling water, until tender; drain. Rinse under cold water; drain. Place noodles in medium bowl; cover, refrigerate until required.
2 Meanwhile, combine mirin, kecap manis, sake, sugar, fresh ginger and garlic in small jug.
3 Cook fish in heated oiled large frying pan until browned both sides and cooked as desired (tuna can become very dry if overcooked; we recommend you sear it over very high heat for about 30 seconds each side). Add mirin mixture to pan; coat fish both sides in mixture. Remove fish from pan; cover to keep warm.
4 Bring mixture in pan to a boil. Reduce heat; simmer, uncovered, 30 seconds. Strain sauce into small jug.
5 Meanwhile, combine nori, onion, oil and pickled ginger in bowl with soba. Divide fish among plates, drizzle with sauce; top with soba mixture. Serve with wasabi paste, if you like.

prep + cook time 25 minutes **serves** 4
nutritional count per serving 10.1g total fat (3.7g saturated fat); 1400kJ (335 cal); 14.9g carbohydrate; 40.8g protein; 3.1g fibre; 443mg sodium; medium GI

This is a great recipe (both the rice and the mince mixture) to cook in large batches, ready to freeze in user-friendly portions.

chilli con carne

⅓ cup (65g) brown long-grain rice
1 small brown onion (80g), chopped finely
1 clove garlic, crushed
180g (5½ ounces) lean minced (ground) beef
1 teaspoon ground cumin
1 teaspoon dried chilli flakes
410g (13 ounces) canned diced tomatoes
2 tablespoons tomato paste
½ cup (125ml) water
125g (4 ounces) canned four-bean mix,
  rinsed, drained
2 tablespoons low-fat natural yogurt
¼ cup coarsely chopped fresh flat-leaf parsley

1 Cook rice in medium saucepan of boiling water until tender; drain.
2 Meanwhile, heat oiled medium frying pan; cook onion and garlic, stirring, until onion softens. Add beef and spices; cook, stirring, until beef is browned.
3 Add undrained tomatoes, paste and the water; bring to the boil. Reduce heat; simmer, covered, 10 minutes. Uncover; simmer about 10 minutes or until mixture thickens slightly. Stir in beans.
4 Serve rice and chilli con carne topped with yogurt. Sprinkle with parsley.

prep + cook time 40 minutes **serves** 2
nutritional count per serving 7.8g total fat (2.8g saturated fat); 1563kJ (374 cal); 43.3g carbohydrate; 27.8g protein; 8g fibre; 378mg sodium; medium GI

veal and fennel rolls with horseradish mash

2 teaspoons olive oil
2 cloves garlic, crushed
2 small fennel bulbs (400g), sliced thinly
3 flat mushrooms (240g), sliced thickly
½ cup (125ml) dry white wine
1 cup (250ml) water
6 veal steaks (600g)
2 tablespoons wholemeal plain (all-purpose) flour
½ cup (125ml) salt-reduced chicken stock
1 tablespoon finely chopped fresh flat-leaf parsley

HORSERADISH MASH
600g (1¼ pounds) potatoes, chopped coarsely
1 tablespoon horseradish cream
¾ cup (180ml) hot low-fat milk
2 tablespoons finely chopped fresh
  flat-leaf parsley

1 Heat half the oil in large frying pan; cook garlic and fennel, stirring, until fennel softens. Add mushrooms, half the wine and ½ cup (125ml) of the water; bring to the boil. Reduce heat; simmer, uncovered, about 15 minutes or until liquid has evaporated. Cool 10 minutes.
2 Meanwhile, using meat mallet, gently pound veal steaks, one at a time, between pieces of plastic wrap until about 5mm (¼ inch) thick; cut each piece in half crossways. Divide fennel mixture among veal pieces; roll to enclose filling, securing each roll with a toothpick.
3 Make horseradish mash.
4 Toss veal rolls in flour; shake off excess. Heat remaining oil in same cleaned frying pan; cook rolls, in batches, until browned all over and cooked as desired. Remove from pan, cover to keep warm. Add remaining wine and water to same pan with stock; bring to the boil, stirring. Boil, uncovered, 5 minutes.
5 Serve the veal with mash and sauce, sprinkled with parsley.

HORSERADISH MASH Boil, steam or microwave potato; drain. Mash potato in large bowl; stir in horseradish and milk, then parsley.

prep + cook time 1 hour 10 minutes serves 4
nutritional count per serving 7g total fat
(1.8g saturated fat); 1492kJ (357 cal);
23.7g carbohydrate; 40.9g protein;
6.1g fibre; 392mg sodium; medium GI

serving suggestion Serve with green salad or steamed green beans.

pasta with tomatoes, artichokes and olives

2 teaspoons olive oil
1 medium brown onion (150g), chopped finely
2 cloves garlic, crushed
¼ cup (60ml) dry white wine
800g (1½ pounds) canned crushed tomatoes
2 tablespoons tomato paste
⅓ cup (40g) seeded black olives
390g (12½ ounces) artichoke hearts in brine, drained, quartered
2 tablespoons coarsely chopped fresh basil
300g (9½ ounces) wholemeal spiral pasta
⅓ cup (25g) finely grated parmesan cheese

1 Heat oil in medium saucepan; cook onion and garlic, stirring, until onion softens. Add wine, undrained tomatoes and paste; bring to the boil. Reduce heat; simmer, uncovered, about 15 minutes or until sauce has thickened. Add olives, artichokes and basil; stir until hot.
2 Meanwhile, cook pasta in large saucepan of boiling water, until tender; drain.
3 Combine pasta and sauce in large bowl. Serve pasta topped with cheese.

prep + cook time 40 minutes **serves** 4
nutritional count per serving 6.8g total fat (1.9g saturated fat); 1668kJ (399 cal); 58.9g carbohydrate; 15.7g protein; 13.1g fibre; 574mg sodium; low GI

brown fried rice with omelette

1⅓ cups (265g) brown long-grain rice
1 tablespoon peanut oil
3 eggs, beaten lightly
2 cloves garlic, crushed
3cm (1-inch) piece fresh ginger (15g), grated finely
1 fresh long red chilli, chopped finely
1 small red capsicum (bell pepper) (150g), cut into
   1cm (½-inch) pieces
115g (3½ ounces) baby corn, cut into
   1cm (½-inch) pieces
100g (3 ounces) green beans, trimmed, cut into
   1cm (½-inch) pieces
100g (3 ounces) fresh shiitake mushrooms,
   sliced thinly
2 tablespoons salt-reduced soy sauce
2 tablespoons rice vinegar
½ cup (40g) bean sprouts, trimmed
4 green onions (scallions), sliced thinly

1 Cook rice in large saucepan of boiling water, until tender; drain. Cool.
2 Heat half the oil in wok; pour in half the egg, tilt wok to coat with egg. Cook until omelette is set. Remove omelette; roll tightly. Repeat with remaining egg. Slice omelettes thinly.
3 Heat remaining oil in wok; stir-fry garlic, ginger and chilli until fragrant. Add vegetables and stir-fry until tender.
4 Add rice, sauce, vinegar and sprouts; stir-fry until hot. Stir in half the onion.
5 Serve rice topped with remaining onion and omelette strips.

prep + cook time 45 minutes (+ cooling) **serves** 4
nutritional count per serving 10.7g total fat
(2.3g saturated fat); 1705kJ (408 cal);
60g carbohydrate; 14.5g protein;
5.9g fibre; 411mg sodium; medium GI

Rice can be cooked the day before; store, covered, in the fridge.

You need a small iceberg lettuce for this recipe.

beef fajitas

600g (1¼ pounds) beef rump steak
16 x 16cm (6-inch) flour tortillas
1 large red capsicum (bell pepper) (350g),
  sliced thinly
1 large green capsicum (bell pepper) (350g),
  sliced thinly
1 large yellow capsicum (bell pepper) (350g),
  sliced thinly
1 large red onion (300g), sliced thinly
3 cups finely shredded iceberg lettuce
1 cup (120g) coarsely grated reduced-fat
  cheddar cheese

FRESH TOMATO SALSA
3 medium tomatoes (450g), seeded, chopped finely
1 medium red onion (170g), chopped finely
1 tablespoon finely chopped drained
  jalapeño chillies
¼ cup finely chopped fresh coriander (cilantro)
1 tablespoon lemon juice

1 Preheat oven to 180°/350°F.
2 Make fresh tomato salsa.
3 Cook beef on heated oiled grill plate (or grill or
barbecue) until cooked as desired. Cover beef;
stand 10 minutes, then slice thinly.
4 Wrap tortillas in foil; heat in oven about
10 minutes or until warmed through.
5 Meanwhile, cook capsicum and onion on same
grill plate, until vegetables are tender.
6 Divide beef and vegetables among tortillas. Top
with lettuce, cheese and fresh tomato salsa; roll to
enclose filling.

FRESH TOMATO SALSA Combine ingredients in
a medium bowl.

prep + cook time 50 minutes serves 8
nutritional count per serving 8.8g total fat
(3.3g saturated fat); 1258kJ (301 cal);
27.4g carbohydrate; 26.1g protein;
3.8g fibre; 337mg sodium; low GI

fish and oven-roasted chips

5 small potatoes (600g)
1 teaspoon sea salt
½ teaspoon cracked black pepper
cooking-oil spray
4 x 120g (4 ounces) firm white fish fillets
2 tablespoons rinsed, drained baby capers
1 tablespoon finely chopped fresh dill
1 teaspoon finely grated lemon rind
⅓ cup (80ml) lemon juice
1 medium lemon (140g), cut into wedges

CITRUS SALAD
1 medium orange (240g), peeled, segmented
1 lebanese cucumber (130g), chopped coarsely
40g (1½ ounces) each baby spinach and
   rocket (arugula) leaves
1 tablespoon white wine vinegar

1   Preheat oven to 220°C/425°F. Oil large baking dish.
2   Halve unpeeled potatoes lengthways; cut each
half into six wedges. Combine potato, in single
layer, in dish with salt and pepper; spray lightly with
cooking-oil spray. Roast about 45 minutes or until
browned lightly and tender.
3   Meanwhile, make citrus salad.
4   Cook fish in large heated oiled frying pan until
browned both sides and cooked as desired.
5   Serve fish drizzled with combined capers, dill,
rind and juice. Serve with chips, citrus salad and
lemon wedges.

CITRUS SALAD Combine ingredients in
a medium bowl.

prep + cook time 55 minutes serves 4
nutritional count per serving 7g total fat
(2.2g saturated fat); 1141kJ (273 cal);
21.4g carbohydrate; 27.7g protein;
3.7g fibre; 169mg sodium; medium GI

We used bream fillets in this recipe but you can use
other firm white fish, such as whiting or john dory.

Risoni is a small rice-shaped pasta very similar to orzo; you can use either for this recipe.

grilled lamb cutlets with pumpkin risoni salad

1 clove garlic, crushed
1 tablespoon finely chopped fresh oregano
1 tablespoon finely chopped fresh chives
2 tablespoons lemon juice
¼ cup (60ml) dry white wine
12 french-trimmed lamb cutlets (700g)

PUMPKIN RISONI SALAD
500g (1 pound) pumpkin, cut into 3cm
  (1¼-inch) pieces
1 clove garlic, crushed
1 tablespoon olive oil
1 cup (220g) risoni pasta
150g (4½ ounces) baby spinach leaves
2 tablespoons lemon juice
2 tablespoons coarsely chopped fresh chives
2 tablespoons fresh oregano leaves

1 Combine garlic, oregano, chives, juice and wine in large bowl, add lamb; toss to coat lamb in marinade. Cover, refrigerate 1 hour.
2 Meanwhile, make pumpkin risoni salad.
3 Drain lamb; discard marinade. Cook lamb on heated oiled grill plate (or grill or barbecue) until cooked as desired. Serve cutlets with risoni salad.

PUMPKIN RISONI SALAD Preheat oven to 200°C/400°F. Place pumpkin, in single layer, on oven tray; drizzle with combined garlic and half of the oil. Roast about 20 minutes or until tender. Meanwhile, cook pasta in large saucepan of boiling water until tender; drain. Combine pasta and spinach in large bowl with pumpkin, juice, herbs and remaining oil.

prep + cook time 50 minutes (+ refrigeration)
serves 4
nutritional count per serving 11.5g total fat (3.6g saturated fat); 1735kJ (415 cal); 46.4g carbohydrate; 28g protein; 5.4g fibre; 73mg sodium; low GI

serving suggestion Serve with steamed green beans and crusty wholemeal bread.

desserts

vanilla ice-cream with mango and berry coulis

¼ cup (30g) custard powder
3 cups (750ml) low-fat milk
½ cup (110g) caster (superfine) sugar
300g (9½ ounces) soft tofu
2 teaspoons vanilla extract

BERRY COULIS
300g (9½ ounces) mixed berries
2 teaspoons icing (confectioners') sugar

MANGO COULIS
1 medium mango (430g), chopped
2 tablespoons water

1 Blend custard powder with a little of the milk in medium saucepan until smooth. Add remaining milk and sugar; cook, stirring, over heat until custard boils and thickens. Remove from heat.
2 Blend or process tofu until smooth. Add tofu and extract to custard; stir to combine. Cool to room temperature.
3 Transfer mixture to 14cm x 21cm (5½-inch x 8½-inch) loaf pan. Cover tightly with foil, freeze 3 hours or overnight.

4 Beat ice-cream in large bowl with electric mixer until smooth. Return to loaf pan, cover; freeze for further 3 hours or until firm. Repeat beating and freezing twice more. Alternatively, churn ice-cream in an ice-cream machine according to the manufacturer's instructions.
5 Make berry and mango coulis.
6 Serve ice-cream with mango and berry coulis.

BERRY COULIS Blend or process berries and sugar until smooth. Push mixture through a fine sieve over small bowl; discard solids.

MANGO COULIS Blend or process mango and the water until smooth.

prep + cook time 40 minutes (+ cooling & freezing)
serves 6
nutritional count per serving 1.4g total fat (0.3g saturated fat); 936kJ (224 cal); 41.2g carbohydrate; 11.1g protein; 2.7g fibre; 90mg sodium; low GI

tip Fresh or frozen berries are suitable; if frozen berries are used they must be thawed before making coulis. Ice-cream and coulis can be made 3 days ahead.

cherry upside-down cakes

425g (13½ ounces) canned seeded black cherries, drained
2 eggs
¾ cup (150g) firmly packed light brown sugar
¾ cup (90g) ground almonds
1 teaspoon vanilla extract
⅓ cup (50g) wholemeal self-raising flour
½ cup (125ml) low-fat milk

1 Preheat oven to 180°C/350°F. Grease 12-hole (⅓-cup/80ml) muffin pan. Divide cherries among pan holes.
2 Beat eggs and sugar in small bowl with electric mixer until light and fluffy. Stir in ground almonds, extract, flour and milk. Spoon the mixture into pan holes.
3 Bake about 20 minutes. Stand 5 minutes before turning, top-side up, onto wire rack to cool.

prep + cook time 40 minutes makes 12
nutritional count per cake 5.1g total fat
(0.6g saturated fat); 568kJ (136 cal);
18.6g carbohydrate; 3.8g protein;
1.4g fibre; 49mg sodium; medium GI

cranberry macerated berries

250g (8 ounces) strawberries, quartered
125g (4 ounces) fresh raspberries
125g (4 ounces) fresh blueberries
1 tablespoon icing (confectioners') sugar
½ cup (125ml) apple, cranberry and pomegranate juice
2 teaspoons finely grated orange rind
½ cup (140g) low-fat vanilla-flavoured yogurt

1 Combine berries, sugar, juice and rind in medium bowl. Cover, refrigerate 3 hours.
2 Serve berry mixture with yogurt.

prep time 10 minutes (+ refrigeration) serves 4
nutritional count per serving 0.3g total fat
(0.1g saturated fat); 422kJ (101 cal);
18.1g carbohydrate; 3.7g protein;
3.9g fibre; 29mg sodium; low GI

tip Any cranberry juice variation would be suitable for this recipe.

citrus salad

1 medium pink grapefruit (425g), segmented
2 medium navel oranges (480g), segmented
1 lime, segmented
60g (2 ounces) strawberries, quartered
½ cup (125ml) unsweetened apple juice
¾ cup (200g) low-fat fruit-flavoured yogurt

1   Combine fruit and juice in medium bowl. Serve
fruit topped with yogurt.

prep time 15 minutes **serves** 2
nutritional count per serving 0.7g total fat
(0.1g saturated fat); 911kJ (218 cal);
40.6g carbohydrate; 8.9g protein;
5.4g fibre; 80mg sodium; low GI

tip If you can't find pink (or ruby) grapefruit, use
regular grapefruit. Any combination of citrus fruit is
fine; mix and match to suit your taste.

baked custard

6 eggs
1 teaspoon vanilla extract
⅓ cup (75g) caster (superfine) sugar
1 litre (4 cups) hot low-fat milk
¼ teaspoon ground nutmeg

1   Preheat oven to 160°C/325°F. Grease shallow
1.5-litre (6-cup) ovenproof dish.
2   Whisk eggs, extract and sugar in large bowl;
gradually whisk in hot milk. Pour custard mixture
into dish; sprinkle with nutmeg.
3   Place ovenproof dish in larger baking dish; add
enough boiling water to baking dish to come
halfway up side of ovenproof dish. Bake about
45 minutes or until set.

prep + cook time 55 minutes **serves** 6
nutritional count per serving 5.6g total fat
(1.8g saturated fat); 836kJ (200 cal);
23.9g carbohydrate; 14.6g protein;
0g fibre; 170mg sodium; low GI

If making individual servings, you need to use eight 1-cup (250ml) disposable cups, otherwise you can use an 8cm x 26cm (3-inch x 10¼-inch) bar cake pan. If using a bar pan instead of the cups, follow the method below, but spread layer into a baking-paper-lined bar pan. Once frozen, slice and serve immediately.

mango, berry and passionfruit frozen yogurt

1 small mango (300g)
250g (8 ounces) strawberries
2 cups (560g) low-fat vanilla-flavoured yogurt
¼ cup (60ml) passionfruit pulp

1 Blend or process half the mango and half the berries, separately, until smooth; finely chop remaining mango and berries.

2 Combine mango puree, chopped mango and ½ cup (70g) of the yogurt in medium bowl; divide mango mixture among eight 1-cup (250ml) disposable cups. Cover, freeze about 1 hour or until surface is firm.

3 Combine strawberry puree, chopped strawberries and ½ cup (70g) of the yogurt in same cleaned bowl; divide strawberry mixture among the cups. Cover, freeze 1 hour or until surface is firm.

4 Combine passionfruit pulp and remaining yogurt in same cleaned bowl; divide passionfruit mixture among the cups. Cover, freeze for 1 hour. Press paddle pop stick firmly into mixture in each cup. Cover, freeze 3 hours or overnight.

5 Remove from cups and serve immediately.

prep + cook time 35 minutes (+ freezing) makes 8
nutritional count per serving 0.2g total fat
(0.1g saturated fat); 343kJ (82 cal);
12.8g carbohydrate; 5.1g protein;
2.1g fibre; 59mg sodium; low GI

rosewater and raspberry jellies

200g (6½ ounces) fresh raspberries
1 cup (250ml) cranberry juice
2 tablespoons caster (superfine) sugar
¼ cup (60ml) water
3 teaspoons powdered gelatine
2 teaspoons rosewater
2 tablespoons reduced-fat pouring cream

1 Blend or process 150g (4½ ounces) of the raspberries until smooth. Stir cranberry juice, sugar and raspberry puree in medium saucepan over medium heat until sugar dissolves. Strain mixture through muslin-lined sieve; discard solids.
2 Place the water in small heatproof jug; sprinkle over gelatine. Stand jug in small saucepan of simmering water, stirring, until gelatine dissolves. Stir rosewater and gelatine mixture into strained raspberry mixture.
3 Divide raspberry mixture among four ½-cup (125ml) glasses. Cover, refrigerate overnight.
4 Serve jellies topped with remaining raspberries; drizzle with cream.

prep + cook time 25 minutes
(+ standing & refrigeration) serves 4
nutritional count per serving 3.2g total fat
(1.8g saturated fat); 502kJ (120 cal);
17.6g carbohydrate; 3.9g protein;
2.7g fibre; 13mg sodium; low GI

For a clear jelly, don't push the mixture through the muslin-lined strainer, instead, allow the mixture to strain gradually.

baked apples with berries

2 cups (300g) frozen mixed berries
4 large apples (800g)
4 cardamom pods
½ cup (140g) yogurt
2 teaspoons honey

1 Place berries in fine sieve set over small bowl,
cover; thaw in refrigerator overnight.
2 Preheat oven to 160°C/325°F.
3 Core unpeeled apples about three-quarters of
the way down from stem end, making hole 4cm
(1½ inches) in diameter. Use small sharp knife to
score around circumference of each apple. Make
small deep cut in base of each apple; insert one
cardamom pod into each cut.

4 Pack three-quarters of the berries firmly into
apples; place apples in small baking dish. Bake,
uncovered, about 45 minutes or until apples are
just tender.
5 Meanwhile, mash remaining berries with a fork
in small bowl; stir in yogurt and honey.
6 Serve apples with yogurt mixture.

prep + cook time 55 minutes (+ refrigeration)
serves 4
nutritional count per serving 1g total fat
(0g saturated fat); 556kJ (133 cal);
25g carbohydrate; 3.9g protein;
4.8g fibre; 35mg sodium; low GI

honey buttermilk ice-cream with fruit salsa

¼ cup (60ml) water
2 teaspoons powdered gelatine
1½ cups (375ml) low-fat evaporated milk
½ cup (175g) honey
1½ cups (375ml) buttermilk

FRUIT SALSA
1 small pineapple (800g), chopped coarsely
1 large mango (600g), chopped coarsely
3 medium kiwifruit (255g), chopped coarsely
250g (8 ounces) strawberries, chopped coarsely

1 Place the water in small heatproof jug; sprinkle over gelatine. Stand jug in small saucepan of simmering water, stirring, until gelatine dissolves.
2 Meanwhile, place evaporated milk in medium saucepan; bring to the boil. Remove from heat; stir in honey and gelatine mixture. Transfer mixture to medium bowl; cool to room temperature.
3 Beat buttermilk in small bowl with electric mixer until frothy; transfer to large jug. Beat evaporated milk mixture in large bowl with electric mixer until light and frothy. Gradually beat in buttermilk until combined.
4 Pour mixture into 2-litre (8-cup) metal container. Cover tightly with foil, freeze 3 hours or overnight.
5 Beat ice-cream in large bowl with electric mixer until smooth. Return to container, cover; freeze for further 3 hours or until firm. Alternatively, churn ice-cream in an ice-cream machine according to manufacturer's instructions.
6 Meanwhile, make fruit salsa.
7 Serve ice-cream with fruit salsa.

FRUIT SALSA Combine ingredients in large bowl.

prep + cook time 50 minutes (+ cooling & freezing)
serves 8
nutritional count per serving 1.4g total fat (0.7g saturated fat); 903kJ (216 cal); 40.8g carbohydrate; 8.8g protein; 3.6g fibre; 88mg sodium; low GI

Tiramisu, translated roughly as "pick-me-up", is usually made from savoiardi (sponge-finger biscuits) soaked in coffee and marsala, then layered with masses of mascarpone and topped with cream. Our version is no less delicious... but far, far less laden with fat!

tiramisu

1 tablespoon instant coffee powder
¾ cup (180ml) boiling water
2 tablespoons marsala
9 sponge-finger biscuits (100g), halved
1 cup (200g) low-fat ricotta cheese
½ cup (120g) light sour cream
2 tablespoons caster (superfine) sugar
2 teaspoons cocoa powder

1 Combine coffee and the water in medium jug; stir in marsala.
2 Stand three biscuit halves upright in each of six ¾-cup (180ml) glasses; drizzle biscuits with the coffee mixture.
3 Beat cheese, sour cream and sugar in small bowl with electric mixer about 4 minutes or until mixture thickens slightly.
4 Divide ricotta mixture among glasses. Cover, refrigerate 3 hours or overnight. Serve dusted with sifted cocoa.

prep + cook time 30 minutes (+ refrigeration)
serves 6
nutritional count per serving 7.9g total fat (4.8g saturated fat); 823kJ (197 cal); 23.1g carbohydrate; 6.1g protein; 0.4g fibre; 189mg sodium; medium GI

serving suggestion Stirring ½ cup pureed fresh strawberries or mango into the ricotta mixture is a nice addition to this dessert.

glossary

ALLSPICE also called pimento or jamaican pepper; tastes like a combination of nutmeg, cumin, clove and cinnamon. Available whole or ground.

BANANA LEAVES used to line steamers and wrap food; sold in bundles in Asian food shops, greengrocers and supermarkets. Cut leaves, on both sides of centre stem, into required sized pieces then immerse in hot water or hold over a flame until pliable enough to wrap or fold over food; secure with kitchen string, toothpicks or skewers.

BARLEY a nutritious grain used in soups and stews (often as a thickener) as well as in whisky- and beer-making. Hulled barley is the least processed form of barley and nutritious and high in fibre. Pearl barley has had the husk discarded and been hulled and polished, much the same as rice.

BASIL
sweet the most common type of basil; used extensively in Italian dishes and one of the main ingredients in pesto.
thai also known as horapa; different from holy basil and sweet basil in both look and taste, having smaller leaves and purplish stems. It has a slight aniseed taste and is one of the identifying flavours of Thai food.

BEETROOT also known as red beets; firm, round root vegetable.

BUCKWHEAT a herb in the same plant family as rhubarb; not a cereal so it is gluten-free. Available as flour; ground (cracked) into coarse, medium or fine granules (kasha) and used similarly to polenta; or groats, which is the whole kernel sold roasted as a cereal product.

BUK CHOY also known as bok choy, pak choi, chinese white cabbage or chinese chard; has a fresh, mild mustard taste. Use stems and leaves, stir-fried or braised. Baby buk choy, also known as pak kat farang or shanghai bok choy, is much smaller and more tender. Its mildly acrid, distinctively appealing taste has made it one of the most commonly used asian greens.

BURGHUL also called bulghur wheat; hulled steamed wheat kernels that, once dried, are crushed into various sized grains. Used in Middle Eastern dishes such as kibbeh and tabbouleh. Is not the same as cracked wheat.

BUTTERMILK in spite of its name, buttermilk is actually low in fat, varying between 0.6 per cent and 2.0 per cent per 100ml. Originally the term given to the slightly sour liquid left after butter was churned from cream, today it is intentionally made from no-fat or low-fat milk to which specific bacterial cultures have been added during the manufacturing process.

CAPERS the grey-green buds of a warm climate (usually Mediterranean) shrub, sold either dried and salted or pickled in a vinegar brine; tiny young ones, called baby capers, are also available both in brine or dried in salt.

CARAWAY SEEDS the small, half-moon-shaped dried seed from a member of the parsley family; adds a sharp anise flavour when used in both sweet and savoury dishes.

CHEESE
cheddar semi-hard, yellow to off-white, sharp-tasting cheese named after the village in Somerset, England in which it was originally produced. For our lower-fat versions we used one with no more than 20 per cent fat.
cottage fresh, white, unripened curd cheese with a grainy consistency and a fat content of 15 to 55 per cent.
cream commonly called philadelphia or philly; a soft cow-milk cheese, its fat content ranges from 14 to 33 per cent.
goat's made from goat's milk, has an earthy, strong taste. Available in soft, crumbly and firm textures, in various shapes and sizes, and sometimes rolled in ash or herbs.
mozzarella soft, spun-curd cheese; originating in southern Italy where it was traditionally made from buffalo's milk. Now generally made from cow's milk, mozzarella is the most popular pizza cheese because of its elasticity and low melting point when heated.
parmesan also called parmigiano; is a hard, grainy cow's milk cheese originating in the Parma region of Italy. The curd for this cheese is salted in brine for a month, then aged for up to 2 years in humid conditions. Reggiano is the best parmesan, aged for a minimum 2 years and made only in the Italian region of Emilia-Romagna.
ricotta a soft, sweet, moist, white cow's milk cheese with a low fat content (8.5 per cent) and a slightly grainy texture. The name roughly translates as "cooked again" and refers to ricotta's manufacture from whey that is by-product of other cheese making.

CHERVIL also known as cicily; mildly fennel-flavoured member of the parsley family with curly dark-green leaves. Available both fresh and dried but, like all herbs, is best used fresh.

CHICKPEAS also called garbanzos, hummus or channa; an irregularly round, sandy-coloured legume used extensively in Mediterranean, Indian and Hispanic cooking. Firm texture even after cooking, a floury mouth-feel and robust nutty flavour; available canned or dried (reconstitute for several hours in water before use).

COCONUT
cream obtained commercially from the first pressing of the coconut flesh alone, without the addition of water; the second pressing (less rich) is sold as coconut milk. Available in cans and cartons at most supermarkets.

milk not the liquid found inside the fruit, which is called coconut juice, but the diluted liquid from the second pressing of the white flesh of a coconut (the first pressing produces coconut cream). Available in cans and cartons.

CUSTARD POWDER instant mixture used to make pouring custard; similar to North American instant pudding mix.

FENNEL also called finocchio or anise; a crunchy green vegetable slightly resembling celery that's eaten raw in salads; fried as a side; or used as an ingredient in soups and sauces.

FLOUR

buckwheat ground kernels of a herb in the same plant family as rhubarb; not a cereal so it is gluten-free.

plain also known as all-purpose; unbleached wheat flour is the best for baking: the gluten content ensures a strong dough, which produces a light result.

self-raising all-purpose plain or wholemeal flour with baking powder and salt added; make yourself with plain flour sifted with baking powder in the proportion of 1 cup flour to 2 teaspoons baking powder.

wholemeal also known as wholewheat flour; milled with the wheat germ so is higher in fibre and more nutritional than plain flour.

GELATINE

we use dried (powdered) gelatine in this book; it's also available in sheet form known as leaf gelatine. A thickening agent made from either collagen, a protein found in animal connective tissue and bones, or certain algae (agar-agar). Three teaspoons of dried gelatine (8g or one sachet) is about the same as four gelatine leaves. The two types are interchangable but leaf gelatine gives a much clearer mixture than dried gelatine; it's perfect in dishes where appearance matters.

HORSERADISH

a vegetable with edible green leaves but mainly grown for its long, pungent white root. Occasionally found fresh in specialty greengrocers and some Asian food shops, but commonly purchased in bottles at the supermarket in two forms: prepared horseradish and horseradish cream.

KUMARA

the Polynesian name of an orange-fleshed sweet potato; good baked, boiled, mashed or fried similarly to other potatoes.

LEMON GRASS

also known as takrai, serai or serah. A tall, clumping, lemon-smelling and tasting, sharp-edged aromatic tropical grass; the white lower part of the stem is used, finely chopped, in much of the cooking of South-East Asia. Can be found, fresh, dried, powdered and frozen, in supermarkets, greengrocers and Asian food shops.

LENTILS

(red, brown, yellow) dried pulses often identified by and named after their colour. Eaten by cultures all over the world, most famously perhaps in the dhals of India, lentils have high food value.

LETTUCE

cos also known as romaine lettuce; the traditional caesar salad lettuce. Long, with leaves ranging from dark green on the outside to almost white near the core; the leaves have a stiff centre rib giving a slight cupping effect to the leaf on either side.

iceberg a heavy, crisp, firm round lettuce with tightly packed leaves.

mesclun pronounced mess-kluhn; also known as mixed greens or spring salad mix. A commercial blend of assorted young lettuce and other green leaves, including baby spinach leaves, mizuna and curly endive.

LSA

is a mixture of ground linseeds, sunflower seed kernels and almonds; available in health-food shops or the health-food section in supermarkets.

MARINARA MIX

a mixture of uncooked, chopped seafood available from fishmarkets and fishmongers.

MARSALA

a fortified Italian wine produced in the region surrounding the Sicilian city of Marsala; recognisable by its intense amber colour and complex aroma. Often used in cooking.

MIRIN

a Japanese champagne-coloured cooking wine, made of glutinous rice and alcohol. It is used expressly for cooking and should not be confused with sake.

MUSHROOMS

button small, cultivated white mushrooms with a mild flavour. When a recipe in this book calls for an unspecified type of mushroom, use button.

flat large, flat mushrooms with a rich earthy flavour, ideal for filling and barbecuing. They are sometimes misnamed field mushrooms, which are wild mushrooms.

shiitake are also known as chinese black, forest or golden oak mushrooms. Although cultivated, they have the earthiness and taste of wild mushrooms. Large and meaty, they can be used as a substitute for meat in some Asian vegetarian dishes.

NOODLES

bean thread also known as wun sen, made from extruded mung bean paste; also known as cellophane or glass noodles because they are transparent when cooked. White in colour (not off-white like rice vermicelli), very delicate and fine; available dried in various size bundles. Must be soaked to soften before use; using them deep-fried requires no pre-soaking.

soba thin, pale-brown noodle originally from Japan; made from buckwheat and varying proportions of wheat flour. Available dried and fresh, and in flavoured (for instance, green tea) varieties; eaten in soups, stir-fries and, chilled, on their own.

NORI

a type of dried seaweed used in Japanese cooking as a flavouring, garnish or for sushi. Sold in thin sheets, plain or toasted (yaki-nori).

POLENTA

also known as cornmeal; a flour-like cereal made of dried corn (maize). Also the dish made from it.

PRESERVED LEMON

whole or quartered salted lemons preserved in a mixture of olive oil and lemon juice and occasionally spices such as cinnamon, clove and coriander. Use the rind only and rinse well under cold water before using.

PROSCIUTTO

a kind of unsmoked Italian ham; salted, air-cured and aged, it is usually eaten uncooked.

RICE

arborio small, round grain rice well-suited to absorb a large amount of liquid; the high level of starch makes it especially suitable for risottos, giving the dish its classic creaminess.

basmati a white, fragrant long-grained rice; the grains fluff up beautifully when cooked. It should be washed several times before cooking.

doongara a white rice with a lower glycaemic index (GI) than most other rices, so it is more slowly absorbed into the blood stream, providing sustained energy release for endurance. Cooks to a firm, fluffy rice, even if it is overcooked.

long-grain elongated grains that remain separate when cooked; the most popular steaming rice in Asia.

short-grain fat, almost round grain with a high starch content; tends to clump together when cooked.

white is hulled and polished rice, can be short-or long-grained.

RICE PAPER ROUNDS also known as banh trang, made from rice paste and stamped into rounds; store well at room temperature. They're quite brittle and will break if dropped; dipped momentarily in water they become pliable wrappers for fried food and uncooked vegetables. Make good spring-roll wrappers.

RISONI small rice-shape pasta; very similar to another small pasta, orzo.

ROLLED BARLEY flattened barley grain rolled into flakes; looks similar to rolled oats.

ROLLED OATS flattened oat grain rolled into flakes and traditionally used for porridge. Instant oats are also available, but use traditional oats for baking.

ROSEWATER extract made from crushed rose petals, called gulab in India; used for its aromatic quality in many sweetmeats and desserts.

SAKE Japan's favourite wine, made from fermented rice, is used for marinating, cooking and as part of dipping sauces. If sake is unavailable, dry sherry, vermouth or brandy can be substituted. If drinking sake, stand it first in a container in hot water for 20 minutes to warm it through.

SAUCES

fish called naam pla on the label if Thai-made, nuoc naam if Vietnamese; the two are almost identical. Made from pulverised salted fermented fish; has a pungent smell and strong taste. Available in varying intensities so use according to your taste.

japanese soy an all-purpose low-sodium soy sauce made with more wheat content than its Chinese counterparts; fermented in barrels and aged. Possibly the best table soy and the one to choose if you only want one variety.

kecap manis a dark, thick sweet soy sauce used in most South-East Asian cuisines. Depending on the manufacturer, the sauces sweetness is derived from the addition of either molasses or palm sugar when brewed.

sweet chilli sweet comparatively mild, fairly sticky and runny bottled sauce made from red chillies, sugar, garlic and white vinegar.

teriyaki a homemade or commercially bottled sauce usually made from soy sauce, mirin, sugar, ginger and other spices; it imparts a distinctive glaze when brushed on grilled meat.

SESAME OIL made from roasted, crushed, white sesame seeds; used as a flavouring rather than a medium for cooking.

SPONGE FINGER BISCUITS also known as savoiardi, savoy biscuits or lady's fingers, they are Italian-style crisp fingers made from sponge mixture.

TOFU also known as soybean curd or bean curd; an off-white, custard-like product made from the "milk" of crushed soybeans. Comes fresh as soft or firm, and processed as fried or pressed dried sheets. Fresh tofu can be refrigerated in water (changed daily) for up to 4 days.

firm made by compressing bean curd to remove most of the water. Good used in stir-fries as it can be tossed without disintegrating. Can also be preserved in rice wine or brine.

silken not a type of tofu but reference to the manufacturing process of straining soybean liquid through silk; this denotes best quality.

soft delicate texture; does not hold its shape when overhandled. Can also be used as a dairy substitute in ice-cream or cheesecakes.

TOMATOES

bottled pasta sauce a prepared tomato-based sauce sometimes called ragu or sugo on the label; comes in varying degrees of thickness and kinds of spicing.

canned whole peeled tomatoes in natural juices; available crushed, chopped or diced, sometimes unsalted or reduced salt. Use undrained.

cherry also known as tiny tim or tom thumb tomatoes; small and round.

egg also called plum or roma, these are smallish, oval-shaped tomatoes much used in Italian cooking or salads.

paste triple-concentrated tomato puree used to flavour soups, stews, sauces and casseroles.

teardrop small yellow pear-shaped tomatoes.

TORTILLA thin, round unleavened bread originating in Mexico; can be made at home or purchased frozen, fresh or vacuum-packed. Two kinds are available, one made from wheat flour and the other from corn.

TZATZIKI Greek yogurt and cucumber dish sometimes containing mint and/or garlic.

VANILLA

bean dried, long, thin pod from a tropical golden orchid; the minuscule black seeds inside the bean are used to impart a luscious vanilla flavour in baking and desserts.

extract obtained from vanilla beans infused in water; a non-alcoholic version of essence.

YOGURT we use plain full-cream yogurt in our recipes unless specifically noted otherwise. If a recipe in this book calls for low-fat yogurt, we use one with a fat content of less than 0.2 per cent.

ZUCCHINI also known as courgette; belongs to the squash family. Flowers can be stuffed or used in salads.

conversion chart

MEASURES

One Australian metric measuring cup holds approximately 250ml; one Australian metric tablespoon holds 20ml; one Australian metric teaspoon holds 5ml.

The difference between one country's measuring cups and another's is within a two- or three-teaspoon variance, and will not affect your cooking results. North America, New Zealand and the United Kingdom use a 15ml tablespoon.

All cup and spoon measurements are level. The most accurate way of measuring dry ingredients is to weigh them. When measuring liquids, use a clear glass or plastic jug with the metric markings.

We use large eggs with an average weight of 60g.

DRY MEASURES

METRIC	IMPERIAL
15g	½oz
30g	1oz
60g	2oz
90g	3oz
125g	4oz (¼lb)
155g	5oz
185g	6oz
220g	7oz
250g	8oz (½lb)
280g	9oz
315g	10oz
345g	11oz
375g	12oz (¾lb)
410g	13oz
440g	14oz
470g	15oz
500g	16oz (1lb)
750g	24oz (1½lb)
1kg	32oz (2lb)

LIQUID MEASURES

METRIC	IMPERIAL
30ml	1 fluid oz
60ml	2 fluid oz
100ml	3 fluid oz
125ml	4 fluid oz
150ml	5 fluid oz
190ml	6 fluid oz
250ml	8 fluid oz
300ml	10 fluid oz
500ml	16 fluid oz
600ml	20 fluid oz
1000ml (1 litre)	1¾ pints

LENGTH MEASURES

METRIC	IMPERIAL
3mm	⅛in
6mm	¼in
1cm	½in
2cm	¾in
2.5cm	1in
5cm	2in
6cm	2½in
8cm	3in
10cm	4in
13cm	5in
15cm	6in
18cm	7in
20cm	8in
22cm	9in
25cm	10in
28cm	11in
30cm	12in (1ft)

OVEN TEMPERATURES

The oven temperatures in this book are for conventional ovens; if you have a fan-forced oven, decrease the temperature by 10-20 degrees.

	°C (CELSIUS)	°F (FAHRENHEIT)
Very slow	120	250
Slow	150	300
Moderately slow	160	325
Moderate	180	350
Moderately hot	200	400
Hot	220	425
Very hot	240	475

The imperial measurements used in these recipes are approximate only. Measurements for cake pans are approximate only. Using same-shaped cake pans of a similar size should not affect the outcome of your baking. We measure the inside top of the cake pan to determine sizes.

BEST SELLERS

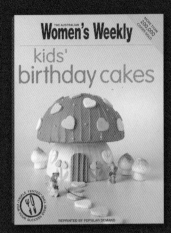

NEW COOKBOOKS

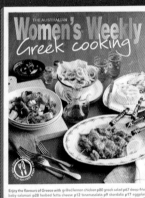
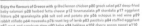

The extensive range of Australian Women's Weekly cookbooks are on sale at selected newsagents and supermarkets or online at www.acpbooks.com.au

Published in 2011 by ACP Books, Sydney

ACP Books are published by ACP Magazines a division of Nine Entertainment Co.

General manager Christine Whiston
Associate publisher Seymour Cohen
Editor-in-chief Susan Tomnay
Creative director & designer Hieu Chi Nguyen
Senior editor Kirsty McKenzie
Food director Pamela Clark
Food editor Nicole Dicker
Sales & rights director Brian Cearnes
Marketing manager Bridget Cody
Senior business analyst Rebecca Varela
Operations manager David Scotto
Circulation manager Sarah Lloyd
Production manager Victoria Jefferys
Circulation manager Sarah Lloyd
Circulation analyst Nicole Pearson

Published by ACP Books, a division of ACP Magazines Ltd, 54 Park St, Sydney; GPO Box 4088, Sydney, NSW 2001.phone (02) 9282 8618; fax (02) 9267 9438.

acpbooks@acpmagazines.com.au;
www.acpbooks.com.au

Printed by Toppan Printing Co, China.

Australia Distributed by Network Services, phone +61 2 9282 8777; fax +61 2 9264 3278; networkweb@networkservicescompany.com.au
United Kingdom Distributed by Australian Consolidated Press (UK), phone (01604) 642 200; fax (01604) 642 300; books@acpuk.com
New Zealand Distributed by Netlink Distribution Company, phone (9) 366 9966; ask@ndc.co.nz
South Africa Distributed by PSD Promotions, phone (27 11) 392 6065/6/7; fax (27 11) 392 6079/80; orders@psdprom.co.za

TITLE: Cooking for diabetes / food director Pamela Clark
ISBN: 978 1 74245 091 9 (pbk.)
Notes: Includes index.
Subjects: Sugar-free diet. Recipes. Cooking
Other Authors/Contributors: Clark, Pamela
Dewey Number 641.563837

Photographer Stuart Scott
Stylist Janelle Bloom
Food preparation Tina Asher, Emma Braz, Lucy Moore
Nutritional information Nicole Dicker, Rebecca Squadrito
Cover Mango, berry and passionfruit frozen yoghurt, page 108

To order books
phone 136 116 (within Australia) or
order online at www.acpbooks.com.au
Send recipe enquiries to:
recipeenquiries@acpmagazines.com.au

Text checked and endorsed by the
Australian Diabetes Council.